Nature's Playthings

NATURE'S PLAYTHINGS

Alison Wilson Smith

MERLIN UNWIN BOOKS

First published in Great Britain by Merlin Unwin Books, 2008

Published by:
Merlin Unwin Books
Palmers House
7 Corve Street
Ludlow
Shropshire SY8 1DB
U.K.

www.merlinunwin.co.uk

The author asserts her moral right to be identified with this work.

Designed and set in Minion Pro by Merlin Unwin
Printed by Leo Paper Products

ISBN 978 1 906122 00 3

CONTENTS

Publisher's note

When Alison Wilson Smith proposed writing a book for us about the joys of playing outdoors, freely, as she did as a child in the 1940s, it seemed a timely proposal – although she had been wanting to do it for years. Now seems a particularly good time to recall the days when children actually walked alone to school, and entertained themselves on the way there and back and throughout the holidays with whatever the seasons provided, from trees to stones to conkers to running streams. All this has changed.

A major report, *Risk and Childhood*, was published by the Royal Society for the Arts* in October 2007, warning that the 'cotton wool' culture is robbing today's youngsters of the freedom to develop, to manage and take risks – and, ultimately, to grow up. It appears that, by trying to protect our children from perceived hazards, we are simply creating new ones. Driving children everywhere increases traffic, making the roads more dangerous; keeping children indoors to avoid criminals is turning them into 'couch potatoes' and they're getting fat; training them to mistrust all strangers is making them introverted and less able to make judgements.

A letter to the *Daily Telegraph* last autumn, signed by author Philip Pullman, environmental campaigner Sir Jonathan Porritt, child-care expert Dr Penelope Leach, not to mention the Chief Executives of The Children's Society, Barnardo's and the Royal Institution, stated that disturbing trends in increased childhood depression and poor health were caused, as a key factor, by 'the marked decline over the past 15 years in children's play'.

* www.rsa.org.uk

'Playing – particularly unstructured, loosely supervised play outdoors – is vital. It develops a child's physical co-ordination, facilitates social development (making and keeping friends, dealing with problems, working collaboratively) and cultivates creativity, imagination and emotional resilience. This includes the growth of self-reliance, independence and personal strategies for dealing with challenging or traumatic experiences.' They called for 'public dialogue about the value of play in children's healthy development and how we can ensure its place at the heart of 21st-century childhood.'

Of course the author of this book, Alison Wilson Smith, did not have any such 'agenda' when she wrote this book – she simply wanted to share the joys of nature's playthings with the next generation of children, who, given half the chance, know instinctively that playing outdoors is fun!

Karen McCall
Merlin Unwin Books
December 2007

INTRODUCTION

After seventy years of chaotic up-and-down life, some of my memories are black and white and others are multicoloured. My childhood has vivid patches, chronologically random and geographically confused. We kept moving (it was wartime) but I was a young child within a family so stability moved with me. I was largely unaware of larger happenings and my world was up close.

I wasn't short-sighted but I liked things up close and stationery. I wanted to examine them, smell them, touch them, play with them, dissect them, make things from them. Mostly it wasn't in the countryside so my free gifts came from small gardens, sparse neighbourhood woodland and local scrubland.

In this book, I want to try to capture the fun, the creativity and the techniques of those innocent, outdoor, utterly absorbing interactions with things which just happened to be around, free for all, often achingly beautiful or absorbingly interesting. They are still there, folks!

I want to record lovely memories from my childhood, and from my childrens', friends' and grandchildrens' childhoods. The fascinating outdoors – whether town, suburbs, country or seaside – were playing and learning grounds to beat all others, giving children a chance to imagine, to be in charge of their own small areas, to absorb the weather, the seasons and nature into their beings as a foundation for the rest of their lives, amusing themselves by themselves or with their friends.

Alison Wilson Smith
Cambridge
December 2007

If you have any memories of your own wonderful outdoor childhood activities I would love to hear about them:
alisonwilsonsmith@googlemail.com

To my family

Acknowledgements

I am very pleased we have been able to include line drawings by Marat Subkhankulov to assist my explanations – he was a delight to teach at Manor Community College in Cambridge, charming and multi-talented.

A further delight has been the photographs of children in the book: Tierre, Tamika and Tom; Charlie and Hazel; Elfrid, Bridget, Lydia and Vita; Sophie; Cecily and John; Marta, Xander and Robin; Alice and Mary – many thanks to them and to their parents.

Thanks also for the photographic contributions of David Mason (pages 2, 38, 40, 42, 147, 150), Matthew Lloyd (pages 16, 20, 132, 142, 144, 180), Jon Potter (page 140) and Ben Bruges (pages 29, 32, 34, 128, 135, 136, 148, 159).

Finally, I am so grateful to Karen McCall and Merlin Unwin, for their unstinting, sympathetic support and free-flowing advice – I would have been lost without their help.

O why do you walk through the fields in gloves
Missing so much and so much?

Frances Cornford, poet and grand-daughter of Charles Darwin

SPRING

Some ideas for spring

- Laurel leaf game
- King of the castle
- Pond dipping
- Leaf boats
- Pooh sticks
- Clay pots
- Stone skimming
- One potato, two potato
- Dams and bridge building
- Stick-in-the-mud
- Puddle jumping
- Cowpat frisbees
- Cherry ear-rings
- Apple peel game
- Fairy pillows
- Dowsing

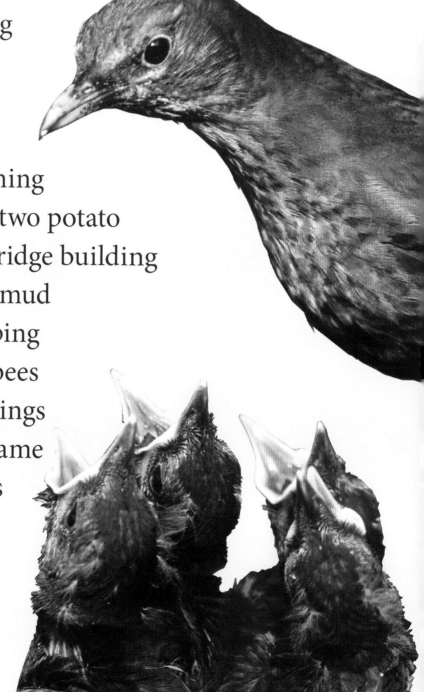

SPRING

I was born in 1938, so my early childhood was dominated by the war – although I was too young to realise that what was happening was in any way unusual.

For long periods of time, chronologically hazy in my mind and broken by family retreats to rural safety and evacuation to Yorkshire and Newcastle, I attended a primary school in Kent, following my two older sisters. It was a fabulous school, led by Mr Thomas, a grand-looking, white-haired Welshman.

Spring runs officially from the Vernal Equinox to the Summer Solstice, tasty words which lisp round the front of your mouth. In other words, spring is from March 20th/21st to round about June 24th although this doesn't make sense because the latter date is Midsummer Day, therefore in the middle of summer, logically? Generally spring is roughly the months March, April and May, which is accurate enough for me.

3

Laurel leaf game

We entered our school via three long parallel pathways, the central one for cars, divided from each other by tall (to us) laurel hedges. As we became older and noticed boys and girls were different, we used laurel leaves for a 's/he-loves-me, s/he-loves-me-not' ritual. We'd find a particularly waxy, shining leaf and, privy only to close friends, secretly scratch onto it the first name of our current heart-throb. Then we'd slip the leaf into a shoe, under the instep but outside the sock. We'd hobble uncomfortably round on this all day.

At home-time (if we'd had the patience to wait that long) the leaf would be carefully extricated and examined in the presence of only the closest of friends. If the name had gone rusty brown, s/he loved us! Looking back, of course they all went brown – from our hot little feet, so it was a pretty safe adventure in fortune-telling.

How to make a laurel leaf love predictor

1. Pick a large, flawless laurel leaf
2. Scratch on the name of your beloved
3. Place under your foot between sock and shoe
4. Leave all day
5. Check it at end of day – a name turned rusty brown means that your love is returned!

Hill play

I like March, the warlike piebald month of blustering wind and driving rain with magical shafts of unexpected sunshine. Named appropriately after Mars, the Roman god of war, March is an exhilarating time to be outside.

As a child, I found it exciting to stand on a hill in a wind so strong it almost blew me over – it felt like flying, that most unattainable desire of childhood. Or you could roll down a hill or run down it so fast your legs looked like a Disney cartoon character.

King of the castle

It just needs a small grassy mound and a few children to play that simple satisfying game of assumed superiority, King of the Castle. One child is chosen to start on top of the mound, singing loudly:

I'm the king of the castle
You're the dirty rascal
I'm the king of the castle
Get down, you dirty rascal!

while the others attempt to lay siege to the castle, at risk of being pushed back down the hill. The one who succeeds in dethroning the monarch then becomes the rightful heir and it all starts again.

Dips

To choose the original king probably involved one of those ancient, esoteric 'dips' or counting-out rhymes, such as this simple one, my favourite, counted out by hitting closed fist on top of closed fist:

One potato, two potato, three potato, four
Five potato, six potato, seven potato MORE!

Or this common one:

> *Dip, dip dip, my little ship,*
> *sailing on the water*
> *like a cup and saucer*
> *O–U–T spells OUT!*

said often in chorus while one child touches the outstretched hands of the other children one by one at each word of the rhyme, culminating in expulsion for the one whose hand receives the ultimate OUT! and then round the circle again until there's no-one left.

And one more much-used one:

> *Eeny meeny miny moe*
> *Catch a tiger by a toe*
> *If he hollers let him go*
> *Eeny meeny miny moe*

Oh no, not a family walk!

March is a good month for long walks because the weather has warmed up a bit and nature is visibly stirring. I only encountered the UK's amazing network of long distance footpaths as an adult, signposted by the acorn silhouette painted on fingerposts and stiles.

A family walk along a short stretch of one of these, or along any marked footpath, is a chance to see lanes and fields close

up, with their trees and flowers, animals and insects, taking advantage of the privileged network of rambling paths spreading an ever more finely-meshed network over Great Britain and round its glorious coasts. It is fascinating to find a panoramic view of rolling countryside and notice the contours, the underlying bony skeleton of the soft hills and valleys.

As always, the internet provides detailed information, or a local ordnance survey map, a treasure in itself, will guide through farm yards and over bridges, wherever there's a right of way created over the years by others walking the same route.

At various points in this book, I will describe items in nature's larder – little edible treats which enhance any walk – as they become available with each majestic turn of the season.

I remember family walks as a child, even during the war, so I must have been very young. I'm not sure I saw the point of them then, although I enjoyed being with my parents and sisters I expect. I was once congratulated on 'walking so far on such little legs' but whether this was one mile or ten I have no idea – I expect because I was the youngest someone was flattering me to keep me stumping along.

Nibbling sorrel

On that or a similar walk I was introduced to the taste of the refreshing, bitter leaves of woodland sorrel for the first time and thereafter lagged behind in my search for these tiny, edible sorrel treasures, like bright

green clover but with finer, slightly folding leaves – in the hedgerows, under trees and growing in crevices of country walls.

On another family walk, through the pine trees of a Forestry Commission development somewhere, with piles of huge logs to climb and sit on and cushioning pine needles underfoot, I remember eating cold baked bean sandwiches – which were delicious in fact but presumably seen as austere war-time fare.

SPRING WATERS

I have lived near a river twice in my life, and sometimes near enough to a stream in a wood. By April, the weeping willows beside a river are cascading their pale green hair down to touch the water as early leaves blur their delicate outlines.

To have the chance to be 'messing about in boats' like Rat and Mole in *The Wind in the Willows*, and glide under the secret canopy of a weeping willow, hidden from the world in its green depths, must be one of the delights of a riverside childhood.

Dam and bridge building

Water for children is like string – an essential. In, on, under or with water – the possibilities are endless: a stream of clear, rippling water, under the trees, with stick and stones, leaves and flowers to play with – paradise; ice-cold bare-foot paddling on a hot day, with mud squidging between the toes; feeling adventurous balancing across stepping-stones you've put there yourself; laboriously building a dam only to see the stream trickle through unhindered…

Bold creative children with a broad enough stream may even find suffi- cient fallen branches to tie together with string or rope (another useful piece of child equipment – imagine swings, and taking 'prisoners') to fashion a raft, which will surely up-end or fall apart and deposit them shrieking and laughing into the water.

A stream un-stoppers the imagination of the most prosaic child: fantasies and fairy tales, physics and mechanics, boat-building and snail-racing, are all on tap and for free.

If you sit quietly by the stream and just watch, you are sure to see those darting jewelled masterpieces, dragonflies: transparent pairs of wings in vivid enamelled greens, blues, gold, all colours, vibrate as they jet around in pursuit of a meal of midges. If you are able to look closely, notice their compound eyes – apparently up to 30,000 facets give them close to 360° of vision, where we poor mortals cope with a measly 180°!

Pond dipping

Whatever the season, water is an endlessly creative element for children of any age or temperament. Pond-dipping is one of the more structured activities but is great, messy fun. It is sometimes teacher-led but it is easy to manage at home, given a pond nearby and either adult supervision, a very shallow pond, or very sensible children!

It is easy and inexpensive to equip for pond dipping: a simple fishing net from a toy shop, or one created from tights or muslin fixed on a wire coat hanger hoop and tied to a stick, or a sieve or a colander; a white ice cream container to show up small creatures; a clear jar for more detailed observation (you can buy them with a magnifying top, very classy); a magnifying glass; a simple reference book; a notebook and pen if you want to take notes.

To dip a pond is easy. Fill your two containers with pond water, to have somewhere ready for your treasures so they are not left gasping and stranded while you hurriedly get life-saving water. Sweep the net steadily through the top few inches at the surface of the pond, being careful not to fall in. Peer into the net and gently empty anything worth looking at more closely into the white container, without hurting any creatures, however small. You may want to transfer, for example, a water snail or some other interesting-looking animal into the clear container to study it with the magnifying glass, perhaps referring to your pocket reference book or making a quick sketch to look up details later on the internet or in a more informative tome. Always put everything back into the pond carefully!

Pond dipping equipment

1. Fishing net from toyshop or one made from muslin on coat hanger wire or sieve/colander tied to stick etc
2. White ex-ice cream container
3. Clear glass/plastic jar (can be bought with magnifying top)
4. Magnifying glass
5. Simple reference book
6. Note pad and pen/pencil

Method

1. Fill both containers with pond water
2. Sweep net through top few inches of pond/rock pool
3. Empty anything vaguely interesting into white container
4. Sweep again a couple of times
5. Transfer anything especially interesting into clear container
6. Study with magnifying glass, take notes, sketch etc
7. Look up in reference book if applicable
8. Carefully return any living specimens back into the pond or rock pool, without hurting them

Tadpoles

The first creatures we all associate with pond dipping are surely tadpoles. Most children have the chance to watch taddies change into frogs; certainly as a small child I would welcome each year the small black commas in an aquarium on the classroom nature table, and look daily (and mostly in vain) for legs to appear – it always happened when our backs were turned or over a weekend or half-term!

Let Nature be your teacher.

William Wordsworth

I recall that frogspawn in a pond is found in clumps whereas toadspawn is in long strings. There is much information on the internet with advice on how to look after these fascinating creatures if you want to watch the life-change at home, or of course in knowledgeable books.

There may be minnows (tiddlers) to catch or fresh water sticklebacks (wonderful name). Newts, like frogs and toads, are amphibian (a lovely concept for children to learn, that these creatures live both on land and in water) and may be found in a pond. The crested newt is the rare variety which is, sadly, an endangered species. It is so important and so useful for children to learn to treat all these creatures with care, to learn

from them directly, and then return them unharmed to their native habitats. Lessons learned thus, with muddy wellies and water running up the sleeves, with shrieks of 'look what I've found!' and 'whatever is this?' will never be forgotten.

I remember seeing my first water-boatman skidding across the surface of a pond, and was fascinated to learn later on that they swim upside-down, two long legs acting as oars propelling them over the surface. They seem so friendly, and so aptly named.

I have one horror story gleaned from a friend: as a child, she and her friends collected tiddlers from their local pond and took them home – where they fried them in butter and had them on toast… Do not do this at home!

Any water – ponds, streams or rock pools – are teeming with life
(*Above*: a bullhead from a stream)

WOODLAND CREATURES

I was never sure if I liked woodlice or not. Their under-the-stone greyness was off-putting but to see them roll up to protect themselves like tiny marbles made them fascinating – it was possible gently to send them rolling along in the dust. When not rolled up, woodlice scuttle – and scuttling is not an attractive way to move.

The kings of scuttling are centipedes and millipedes. Once I learned that any word with 'cent' in probably meant a hundred somethings, and 'mille' a thousand somethings, I started trying to count the legs of these, the most speedy of all UK insects. Of course they are just nicknames, not accurate counts, but they do have lots of scurrying, flicking little legs working away on each side as they dart around. Centipedes are smaller, and have one pair of legs per segment of their creepy arthropod bodies where millipedes have two pairs per segment. I had to learn that an arthropod was any kind of creature with a segmented exoskeleton, appendages from each segment – ugh, creatures of horror films!

How much more loveable and beloved are ladybirds! Perhaps because they are pretty, perhaps because any child can persuade a ladybird to crawl onto a finger and the child can cry

'Ladybird, ladybird, fly away home!
Your house is on fire, your children alone.'

and watch the ladybird open its scarlet spotted wing-cases revealing the delicate lacy transparent brown true wings underneath, and fly away. They are beloved by adult gardeners too since they feed on the dreaded aphids infesting the roses.

I was never arachnophobic – frightened of spiders.

Weaving spiders, come not here;
Hence, you longlegged spinners, hence!

sang Shakespeare's first fairy, protecting her queen, Titania, in *A Midsummer Night's Dream* but I found them skilful and interesting. My only childish habit involving spiders I still indulge – if I see a tiny so-called money spider I still carefully take it on my finger, circle it two or three times above my head and then let it run into my hair! This extraordinary manoeuvre is meant to guarantee wealth but it certainly hasn't so far…and I've no idea what happens next to the spider.

Just to finish on creeping things, as a child I did not encounter many snakes – but then we have very few in Britain. I learned we had mostly non-poisonous ones like slow worms, which are of course not snakes at all but leg-less lizards and totally harmless. Our only venomous snake is an adder, identified by the inverted V on its neck, if a snake can be said to have a neck, which helps us to remember its other name of viper. I only came across this rhyme, rather than the living beast:

> *Why did the viper vipe her nose?*
> *Cos the adder add 'er 'anky!*

which small me found hilarious and endlessly repeatable.

Stag beetles

Beetles are fascinating creatures. I was never especially hooked on bugs, as many children are – I suppose I preferred the more static botanic side of things – but I loved stag beetles, which some children would race for fun, not hurting them at all, I hope.

I remember one particular friend and I – we were about twelve – had a special stream in a woodland which we would visit for the purpose of finding stag beetles in the rotting undergrowth, and crayfish in the stream. Sadly those monstrous gothic stag beetles, sometimes 8 centimetres in length, shiny black-brown and Britain's largest insect, are globally threatened, with the UK its most important remaining sanctuary. Here the beetle is a protected species, with schemes all over the country asking the public to report sightings and protect its environment by not clearing away rotting undergrowth and fallen trees.

A stag beetle looks fearsome and has the reputation of summoning thunder and lightning, which may be why some people react by stamping on them – but the male is harmless to humans. Its huge jaws, which look like antlers, are useless for biting and only useful to frighten off other males. So, folks, join in the surveying and protection activity of this wonderful insect, details as always on the internet!

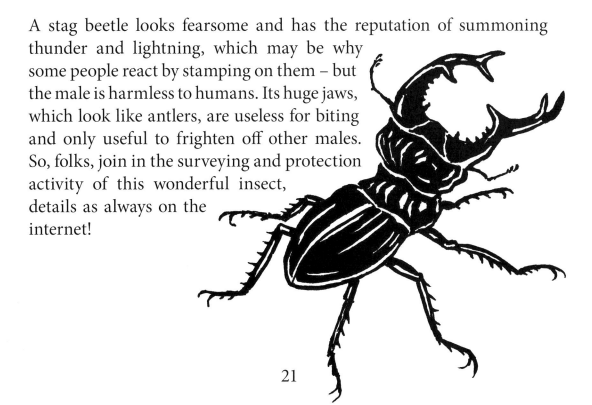

Leaf boats

Leaf boats are so simple to make, and enchanting to watch. Any large, broad leaf will do – look for stinging nettles and you'll find some dock leaves nearby (odd, that, but useful, since a dock leaf scrubbed hard on a nettle sting until the afflicted flesh turns green with the juice will ease that painful, hot itching). Dock leaves work well because they are big, with a strong central rib; two leaves together will make a fragile boat, with the smaller of the two upright for a sail.

A more sea-worthy vessel can be made using a piece of a small branch for the boat, with a broad leaf poked in creating the sail, or if you are lucky enough to have scrounged or found a cork from a wine bottle, a leaf sail or two on this will create a splendid vessel.

It's exciting to race leaf boats against each other or against your friend's, especially if there are miniature waterfalls and treacherous eddies to navigate. Some courageous souls had beetle passengers and crew (without hurting them at all and freeing them afterwards) on their boats but I never rose to such heights.

Growing cress

Remember those primary school nature tables? That magic of writing a name or drawing a simple pattern with mustard and cress seeds on a piece of damp flannel and watching the steady green growth until it was big enough to take home to add to salads – do they still do that?

Another variation is to fill an empty yoghurt pot with damp cotton wool, painting on a face, and sprinkling mustard and cress seeds on which will grow into an attractive green 'afro' crowning a mustard-and-cress-man.

Stone skimming

Hours of simple pleasure, competitive if wished, can be enjoyed with some flattish stones and an expanse of water: to learn the knack of skating stones across the water so that they bounce, skid or 'stott' as many times as possible is a skill which gives pleasure well into old age. I was quite good at it, having a tom-boyish style of throwing although I have never managed more than a five or six bounces.

It seems the world current record is fifty-one skatings, which seems quite incredible – with the luscious prize of a bag of fudge!

Wherever there is water, people will throw stones and sticks in, generally completely harmlessly – but of course really stupid people will throw in bottles and cans, shopping trolleys and bikes – vandalism of the worst sort, dangerous to humans and wild life. Don't do it, people!

Stone skimming requirements

1. Open water – still sea, pond, lake
2. Flattish stones

Method
1. With sideways movement of arm, stone held between middle finger and thumb, index finger on top to guide, fling stone as hard and as flat as you can so that it bounces, skates, skips or 'stotts' as many times on the surface of the water as possible
2. Try to beat your own score, or your opponent's score

Just to sit quietly by a stream, especially if you were lucky enough to have some sandwiches and a drink, listening to the water over the stones and the wind in the trees, created a tranquillity in a generally noisy world which was healing, nourishing to the soul. There are few more lovely experiences, of the suitably English under-stated kind.

Pooh sticks

Without A. A. Milne, would we have had pooh sticks? Brought up, as I was, on *Winnie the Pooh*, *Alice*, and *Wind in the Willows*, with illustrations by E. H. Shepard and John Tenniel, of course I learned how to play pooh sticks at a very early age. I still find myself playing it, or wanting to, whenever I'm on a bridge over a stream or a river.

It is, of course, very simple and highly competitive: each player, at the words 'ready-steady-go', drops a stick into the water on the upstream side of the bridge. Everyone races screaming to the other side and the person whose stick first appears is the winner – and as sticks are often so similar there will be large arguments as to whose it actually is, and anyway the dropper cheated somehow, which all adds to the fun. Crazily, there is an annual World Pooh Sticks Championships on the Thames near Dorchester. The original A. A. Milne bridge is said to be in Hartfield, East Sussex and is visited by thousands of Winnie the Pooh fans every year.

It goes without saying that every child should learn to swim – for the fun of it, as a competitive sport or just for safety and for the skill to rescue someone or something if that need should arise. I remember being taught to swim in a municipal swimming pool and the confidence that gave me to swim (sensibly, with people around) in the sea, river or lake.

Pooh sticks requirements

1 At least one companion
2 Both (or all) to have identifiable sticks
3 A bridge over running water

Method

1 Both (or all) lean over bridge upstream
2 Shout ready-steady-go
3 Drop sticks into water
4 Rush to other side of bridge (watch out for traffic!)
5 See whose stick comes in sight and under the bridge first
6 Loudly proclaim stick's owner the winner!

You can even play Pooh sticks without bridge!

RAIN

While we're talking about water, of course there's rain! I lived in northern Africa for a couple of years where it rained only once a year. I was an adult with a small child and a pregnancy but I cried for wet hedges, for the smell of rain on dusty pavements, for green-ness above all. I still love rain, and refuse to moan about it. Where would our wonderful scenery be without rain?

Splashing and jumping in puddles – what a delight! I'm always mildly sad to see a mother tugging a young child away from a puddle when the longing to splash is manifest in every wriggle, and I love watching the reverse – a shared joyousness as two small feet jump emphatically into the centre of this magic, safe, convenient pool of water, and mother and child squeal with delight at the splashes.

Insy winsy spider
Climbing up the spout
Down came the rain
And washed the spider out
Out came the sun
And dried up all the rain
Insy winsy spider
Climbed up the spout again

Stick-in-the-mud

Water + mud + children = lovely game. Stick-in-the-mud is an international formula. A friend from Panama described to me the intricate contest he and his friends invented with just sticks and mud, called, appropriately, Stick-in-the-mud:

The Rules

You need a deep-ish pool of thick mud and two sticks for two players. I'm going to call them Carlos and Manuel for clarity (Fig 1). Carlos first spears his stick as hard as he can down into the mud. Manuel spears his down next to it as hard as possible to knock out Carlos's stick if he can (Fig 2). If he succeeds, Manuel hits Carlos's stick as far away as possible using his own stick like a baseball (rounders!) bat (Fig 3). While Carlos runs to get his stick, Manuel spears his stick as often as he can in and out of the mud until Carlos gets back, each spearing scoring one point (Fig 4). Let's hope Manuel's and Carlos's mums were all right about the mud… I believe this game illustrates perfectly the point of this book – children will use whatever is to hand when they are freed to do so, costing nothing, making their own fun.

1

MUD

CARLOS   MANUEL

2

3

4

Score: 5

In the gutter

Our house was near the bulbous end of our small close in Kent, a short road of between-the-wars semis. The rounded end had quite a high kerb so when it rained hard this would flood excitingly – of course no fun at all if floodwater entered the houses but it never did.

I can't remember the content of the games our gang of road-urchins created but they were complex, imaginative – and very wet! I have no idea, looking back, how the floods inconvenienced the adults or even what time of the year they occurred or even how often, but our families had the sense to let us get wet and wet again as we passionately played our private games in the brown, cold water.

St Swithin's Day

We learned early on to watch, sceptically of course, if it was going to rain on 15th July, St Swithin's day:

> *St Swithun's day if thou dost rain*
> *For forty days it will remain*
> *St Swithun's day if thou be fair*
> *For forty days 'twill rain na mair*

but always forgot to check afterwards, anyway.

Mud pots

Of course it is also great fun to make pots and plates from mud if you can find the right clay-ey sort, perhaps dug out from a river bank, and have sufficient sunlight to bake them dry or a kind adult with a kiln or an oven. 'Pottery' which just dries naturally is very fragile but still fun to create, whether coiled or thumb pots or pretend plates and boxes.

Thunder and lightning

It was even more exciting to be snug and under cover when there was a thunderstorm! Children can be helped to experience the majestic power of the thunder and the unearthly beauty of the lightning rather than encouraged to be terrified of them. Of course children must be safe, so of course they must be taught not to shelter under the tallest trees around, or stand alone in the middle of a field or be in a boat in the middle of a lake, to protect them from unlikely but possible lightning strikes.

But they can be taught to enjoy, to revel in the utterly harmless but heart-shaking drum-rolls and crashes of thunder, so primitive, such grandeur, like a vast lion roaring up in the clouds.

It is impossible to exaggerate the importance of dens and lairs and hide-outs for children, in my opinion. Of course we must have our children safe but I always believed they need to be able to play out of sight and hearing for their own invention and development – and fun!

How far away is the storm?

The build-up to a thunderstorm is also exciting: stuffy heat but no sun; slow huge raindrops landing as wet patches like saucers; the wind whipping up from somewhere; then the first distant drum-roll.

I learned I could measure 'how far away' a storm was by turning my open palm at the wrist, face-up then face-down, between hearing thunder and seeing lightning – each flick was a mile, I firmly believed. We believed one second (one hand flick) equals one mile away, although I don't know if that's remotely scientific. Then there was the terrifying thrill when there was no gap between thunder and lightning as it crashed directly overhead!

A secret dry place on a wet day

Our 1930s semi had, in common with all the other identical houses in the road, a surprisingly large porch sheltering the front door; for snugness and a secret-telling hideout, nothing could beat having an eiderdown (no duvets had yet reached the UK), some cushions and a friend snuggling warm as the rain pelted down just a few feet away.

My mother obviously knew we were there but because the front door was rarely used, we could pretend we had run away or were on a boat or with Scott (my absolute childhood hero) in the Antarctic. Or just be warm and gossip.

The perfect shelter in a Scottish pine forest

Rain rhymes

Rain has such different characteristics. In Scotland one holiday, it misted with rain all day, every day, gently soaking everything.

The huge great dinner plates of drops as a thunderstorm threatened, on the other hand, could be avoided, if you ran fast enough. Of course rain streaming down a window pane when you were inside, with an open fire and a new book, enhanced the experience no end.

Being such an intrusive substance, rain inevitably gave birth to rhymes. We took great delight in chanting

It's raining, it's pouring,
The old man is snoring,
He went to bed and bumped his head
And couldn't get up in the morning

although who the poor old man was we never knew. People of all ages use the following like a spell, an incantation to bring back the sunshine they craved:

Rain, rain, go away,
Come again another day.

or spitefully

Rain, rain, go away,
Come again on washing day.

or selfishly

Rain on the green grass,
and rain on the tree,
rain on the housetop,
but not on me.

It is said the original couplet appeared around the time of the Spanish Armada, in the form of:

Rain, rain, go to Spain,
Never show your face again

but I can't help thinking it's just the convenient xenophobic rhyme of rain with Spain.

As a child, I loved looking into the sky to detect

a patch of blue sky big enough to make a sailor a pair of
trousers

which definitely meant it would stop raining so that we could play cricket against the lamp post or roller-skate down the road or whatever else we wanted to do with the desperate urgency and impatience of childhood. Or in any season we might look at the sky at sunset and say to each other wisely:

Red sky at night,
Shepherd's delight;
Red sky in the morning,
Shepherd's warning

Dowsing

I tried water divining or dowsing a few times as a child with a Y-shaped hazel twig but I was terrified it might work and glad when it didn't. It would, however, seem that many people *do* have the knack to find underground water by this method if they try.

Water divining or dowsing: how it's done

Requirements
1. A Y-shaped twig, preferably hazel.

Method
1. Hold the two prongs of the twig loosely in your hands, thumbs upwards (not as depicted!).
2. Hold the twig parallel with the ground.
3. Walk slowly over the ground – perhaps practicing where you already know there is an underground stream, or a water pipe.
4. The twig will twitch downwards in the presence of water if successful.

He's got the wrong end of the stick!

Rainbows

I still feel breathless when the sun and the rain together create a rainbow. That magical spring light of sun and shadows, rain and shine have an unearthly quality, especially when, for example, a tree in blossom is lit up by a shaft of sunlight against the backdrop of black rain clouds – oh, to be able to paint! The majesty, the sheer out-of-this-world size of a rainbow over-arching our world makes it a holy thing, whether you believe it is a divine promise or not. I learned, when the weather was that strange mixture of rain and shine, to turn my back on the sun to seek the possible rainbow.

Sometimes they are gloriously double, or even further duplicated with the palest colours – are they actually there or just imagined? I was never interested in the scientific refraction-of-light explanation of a rainbow's genesis but I did learn the order of the colours of its spectrum by this mnemonic (a wonderful, ridiculous word, harder to remember or spell than its function of aiding memory):

Red Orange Yellow Green Blue Indigo Violet
Richard Of York Gained Battles In Vain

SPRING STIRRINGS

Spring – a leap up and forward, the very meaning of the word! Let's hope the seasons do not become so blurred in our temperate zone by climate change, global warming or whatever else is happening to our beautiful planet that we no longer experience that excitement as winter loosens its grip, water flows again and green shoots shoot up into the bright, fitful sun.

For children, spring is just the world a bit warmer, brighter, prettier, with more outdoor possibilities, not so cocooned in winter wrappings and bootings.

Birds and nests

March, April, May – these are magical wake-up months in childhood, signalled perhaps above all by the appearance of delicate flowers, trees coming into leaf and birds carrying nest material in their beaks. I always wanted to follow an industrious bird with a beak-full of wispy straw but of course it was always too quick and too secretive for me to find its nest; it couldn't know I meant it no harm and just wanted to observe its home-building close up.

I can remember trying to create an indeterminate bird's nest, the lowest common denominator of nests, from twigs lined with moss and perching it in a bush thinking how happy a tired bird would be to find a pre-fabricated home – but they were never tenanted when I went back to look so there was obviously something wrong with my creation. In one place where we lived we could watch swallows and house martins building their weird nests for all the world like children's mud pies stuck high under an eave – all they needed, it seemed, was a puddle and some mud, just like kids! They feed on the wing so didn't have to be fed by us.

Swallow and chicks

Swans

I remember being in a group of fellow secondary school pupils one spring, watching in horror as a male mute swan on the Thames was apparently drowning a female swan by holding her head under water, only to have it dawn slowly on us that they were mating – and as we looked round, every bird, butterfly and insect seemed to be mating simultaneously, in an abandoned, wild carnival.

Cuckoo

Then there's the cuckoo, whose haunting noise heralds the spring, bestowing and measuring distance across meadows and woodland.

> *Cuckoo, cuckoo, pray what do you do?*
> *In April I open my bill,*
> *In May I sing night and day,*
> *In June I change my tune,*
> *In July away I fly,*
> *In August away I must.*

I don't think I ever saw a cuckoo in the flesh but of course we all learned how it laid an egg in a smaller bird's nest which was hatched and tended by the surrogate mother, the interloper growing huge in comparison, and how the growing chick unceremoniously shuffled out any would-be step-siblings to their deaths. Nevertheless, the cuckoo call is magic and we all tried to identify the change in its tune – every June.

SPRING FLOWERS

Suddenly in spring there was bright colour all around – mostly yellows, blues, purples and white, for some botanical or pollinating reason. In gardens and woods, fields and hedgerows, green shoots, then the leaves proper, then flowers in all their miniature glory appeared again, just as they had the previous spring, and the one before that, as far back as a child could remember. Often that child would know where to look for the annual re-appearance of a favourite flower – beneath a special hedge for pale primroses, the edge of a field for tiny violets, under some trees for shining white wood anemones, also delightfully named windflowers (and I still have to say anemone? anenome? to myself, or even look it up to make sure).

As quite a young child I was given a copy of *Name this Flower* by Gaston Bonnier, happily in English, by an aunt who must have seen my interest in wild flowers. Once I learned the simple terms of a flower's anatomy – petal, sepal, stamen, stigma, style and all – I was thrilled to discover that by a process of detection, fascinating in itself, through the logical pages

of this wonderful book I could identify even the smallest vetch or the tallest cow parsley by colour and anatomical details. I am sad when children cannot recognise common flowers like primroses, celandine, violets, windflowers, tiny wild daffodils, cowslips, kingcups, buttercups, wild scillas – it's all their heritage.

Luckily there are plenty of pocket-sized books with clear pictures and sensible gobbets of text teaching our wild flowers (and birds and trees and fish and mammals and rocks – like *The Guardian*'s wall charts) – so, start giving them as presents, you know it makes sense!

I could – I want to – describe these ethereal spring flowers in detail to illustrate how much I have always loved them but it would not make interesting reading. I must mention a few, however.

Snow drops, drops of snow! The delicacy of the fine green arching stem dangling the tiny white lamp-shade with its inner ring of matching green-edged petals – and how clumsy that description is

45

alongside the flower itself – so get out there, kids, and look for them poking up through the snow or under the trees, and be properly awed.

I didn't see cowslips until I was grown up, for some reason. Having always heard of them, and learned in my school choir to warble Ariel's

> *Where the bee sucks, there lurk I*
> *In a cowslip's bell I lie*
> *There I couch when owls do cry*

William Shakespeare

they always seemed very special, with that cosy miniature of a fairy tucked up to sleep in a cowslip flower head. Enchanted by their greeny-yellow flowers, I didn't probe the name – I was right not to: they are apparently so-called because they frequently grow in the presence of cowpats or cowslips. According to a legend, St Peter dropped the keys to Heaven and where they landed cowslips grew (the flowers were thought to resemble a set of keys) – so, he dropped the keys to Heaven, no less, carelessly in a cowpat. Hmm.

However, tradition says that if you want to be left alone, spread cowslips on your doorstep, or you could split rocks by striking with a cowslip and find fairy gold therein. Hmm again.

Spring isn't spring without daffs. Daffodils suddenly flood the gardens and parks with dancing gold (sorry, Wordsworth). Suburban streets look Japanese and dressed up for spring as blushing pink and immaculate white blossom bedecks the dark branches of their kerbside trees, and then the petals drop to carpet the road. Or we would surreptitiously shake a blossoming tree and cover ourselves with 'confetti', especially loving it if it caught in our hair.

Cowpat frisbees

A down-to-earth friend said she lived on a farm as a child where there was little spare money for entertainment. She and her brother would find a cowpat which had landed and then dried in a perfect circle – and use it as a frisbee… She told me that, as her own daughter grows up, she follows the rule 'the dirtier you are the more fun you've had', and I've every sympathy with that, not least because as you have fun you are developing a tough immunity to all kinds of things.

Cherry ear-rings

Most urban blossoms are ornamental cherry trees, grown for their flowers only. Real cherries for me as a child were bought in a greengrocers, and for several hours we all fancied our Spanish looks as we hung cherry twins over our ears as dramatic ear-rings. Blossom is everywhere – the horse chestnut, future provider of the all-conquering conkers, drips tiny flowers from its candles until there's a summer snowstorm.

Apple peel game

The apple trees in our garden gave me a lesson in patience. First there was the pretty spring blossom, white against the new light green leaves but with a faint tinge of pink. I learned these had to be cross-pollinated so I endured the bees and wasps that buzzed around the flowers.

As the petals fell the middle bit swelled into an apple, with a strengthened stalk at one end to carry the weight of the fruit and what looked like the remains of the flower at the other.

Apple Peel Love Detector

When I was allowed to use a knife, I loved peeling a delicious apple carefully in one continuous peel which I would chuck over my left shoulder; it would form the initial letter of my future husband – much merriment all round as my family identified the name of one of my scruffy street friends and had me blushing scarlet as they pronounced us man and wife together.

Bread and Cheese Tree

Hawthorn or May – there are so many myths, legends and customs associated with this quintessentially spring hedgerow beauty that you will have to look them up for yourselves – they would half-fill this book on their own. It is one of the earliest trees/bushes to leaf in spring; the tiny bright green shoots and leaf buds are so tasty they have given hawthorn the nickname of 'the bread and cheese tree'. The hedges turn white with its blossom then seem to blush pink but it's an optical illusion: the stamens turn red but the petals stay white. They drop, and leave tiny, tiny 'brushes' small enough for a fairy or a really small dolls house.

How can I not write about primroses, my favourite flower? Under a hedge at the edge of a field or in a wood nestling near the bole of a tree, these delicate pale yellow flowers, a colour no other flower has and which is really difficult to reproduce on paper, glow against their serrated, padded rosette of leaves. When I worked as nurse in London and had to give a patient an injection or some other treatment involving discomfort or pain, I always said 'Don't worry, Mr So-and-So, think of primroses' which possibly irritated them no end.

Is there anything more beautiful than a bluebell wood? I'm sure there are other sights as beautiful but I don't see how anyone can fault the breath-taking, luminous blue carpet spreading into the distance under the newly-leafed trees in a peaceful wood dappled with spring sunlight: calendar cliché of course, so English it squeaks – but I still catch my breath and just gaze. I can't see how anything need be more beautiful.

Like many wild flowers, bluebells are a protected species so bulbs must not be up-rooted. Britain has 50% of the world's bluebells so we are globally responsible for this exquisite sight. Scotland, generally wilder and more rugged than England, has nevertheless adopted the delicate version, the exquisite harebell, as the Bluebell of Scotland. Single-belled, on a delicate stem, of the most delicate of lavender-blues, a harebell must just be gazed at and loved.

Catkins: fairy pillows or doll's pets

The soft grey velvety catkins from goat willow have surely given it its more common name, pussy willow – they are so stroke-able! However, there are traditions that give a more detailed explanation: for example, a Polish legend has kittens falling into a river and being saved by a willow sweeping its branches into the water to rescue them. Ever since, the willow branches are tipped with furry buds in spring. It is said fairies use them for pillows: I would say they are perfect for tiny temporary silky grey pets for small dolls.

SUMMER

Some ideas for summer

- Dandelion clock
- He loves me, he loves me not
- Daisy chains
- Buttercup test
- Poppy dolls
- Foxglove thimbles
- Miniature gardens
- Grass whistle
- Acorn whistle
- Owl hooting
- Fake grasshopper
- Rose games
- Plantain soldiers

NO SCHOOL FOR SUMMER!

The year warms up to summer – or it used to, at least: now snow in May, floods in June are becoming common-place. The summers of my childhood were very long and very hot, I know they were. The long, long summer holidays from school stretched on and on and on, heavenly space and time. There was time to do anything and everything.

Few of my immediate 'gang' went away on holiday, probably none went abroad, so we knew that for the next six to eight weeks we would depend on ourselves for entertainment, and how we relished that! We had no responsibilities and we were too young for homework. We lived a modified street life – modified because our street was a modest suburban close with neat front gardens and accessible (if we wanted them) long back gardens. I can remember now that magic feeling of eternity stretching out, waking up on the first morning of the summer holidays.

Dandelion clock

Of course there were flowers everywhere, wild weeds and cultivated. How universal is the dandelion clock? We hadn't a single watch amongst us and although we would pester any passing adult with 'What's the time, please?' ever-mindful of when we had to go in, even if we were going to ignore it, we would also pretend to trust a dandelion clock, roaring with laughter when we all achieved totally different times anyway.

I was thrilled to learn that the name dandelion came from Old French dent-de-lion, lion's tooth, because of the serrated edge of the leaves and I would murmur 'dent-de-lion' to myself, feeling very sophisticated.

Of all plants, the dandelion surely has the most beautiful seed formation, with its perfect globe of fairy-like parachutes as each floweret produces a seed, just waiting for children (or the wind) to blow them away.

Of course everyone knows how to tell the time this way – count one for every puff and whatever number you reach to blow away the last delicate seed is the o'clock time, however unlikely.

How a dandelion clock works

1. Very carefully pick a fully seeded, fluffy dandelion head
2. Count the number of puffs it takes to blow away all seeds on tiny parachutes
3. That number is the time... fairy time, perhaps

DAISIES

He loves me, he loves me not

Who knows how long ago people started using flowers to test the faithfulness of the beloved? I can't remember when I started pulling the petals off an innocent daisy in the traditional way, whispering 'he loves me – he loves me not – he loves me – he loves me not' as each tiny petal sacrifice was flung to the winds. In fact, I can't remember being taught any of the games devised from nature's gifts; we seemed to absorb them by some kind of innate osmosis.

How many petals are there on a daisy? Do all daisies have exactly the same number? We probably chose this many-petalled flower because the very large number gave us a longer time to hope for a happy outcome and no chance to cheat. A mere five-petalled flower would have been no good: if our maths were up to it we could predict the outcome or even manipulate the result in advance, with fate having no part, which was very unsatisfactory and too prosaic – we needed the magic of the daisy.

Daisy chains

I've made daisy chains at all ages – earnestly as a little girl, idly as an older schoolgirl, helpfully as a grandmother. The daisies can be picked as needed while you lie on the grass, sniffing the earth-and-grass smells in the hot sun.

The basic technique is fiddly but simple, provided you have at least one longish finger nail.

Using your nail, you carefully make a small slit in the pinkish stem of a daisy then you carefully thread through the slit the stem of the second daisy until stopped by the flower head.

Daisies don't fade quickly, another of their charms, so the necklace will last until home time or until you are bored with that particular make-believe.

Daisies are such a delight – tiny, modest, ubiquitous, so prettily the classic flower shape of slender petals radiating from a significant centre. It is possible it was originally called the Day's Eye because the flower head opens and closes with daylight and dusk – the white and gold seem appropriate. The flowers are down there, in the grass, at child level and children have surely always played with them. Their prettiness and abundance call out to be turned into decorations – rings, bracelets, necklaces, tiaras and garlands all readily created from the standard daisy chain.

There are two types of daisy chain, depending upon the effect you want to create.

A   If you make the slit right up near the flower head and then thread the second daisy in and pull it through so that the heads lie snugly together and so on with more daisies, you will create an unwieldy and stiff chain which will take a long time to grow.

B   If, like me, you are impatient for the finished article, you will make the tiny slit as far away from the flower head as possible without it leaking off the end and splitting the stem, then thread the next daisy and pull the head through so that the flowers are prettily separated by lengths of stem, continuing the technique until you have a chain fit for a crown or a necklace or whatever you want – and it grows fast!

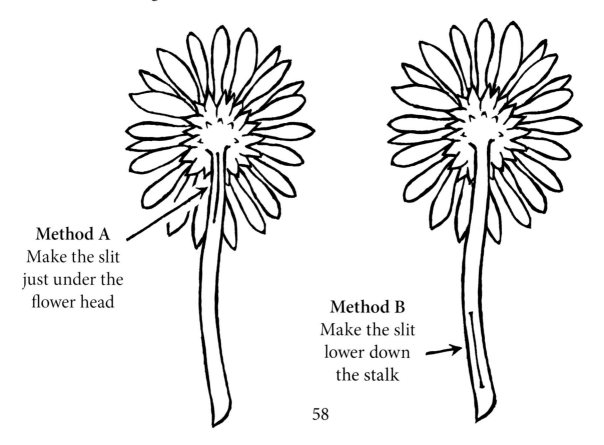

Method A
Make the slit just under the flower head

Method B
Make the slit lower down the stalk

Push the daisy
through the slit
on the stalk

Slide flower heads
together. Now you
are ready for the
next daisy

Buttercups and daisies – one of those classic pairings, like horse and cart, fish and chips. They are seen together in our wonderful meadows, white and gold and green. Another song that stuck in my head from warbling it at school put these two beautiful, modest flowers together in my mind:

As I was going to Strawberry Fair,
Singing, singing, buttercups and daisies,
I met a maiden taking her wares, fol-de-dee.
Her eyes were blue and golden her hair,
As she went on to Strawberry Fair.
Ri-fol, Ri-fol, Tol-de-riddle-li-do,
Ri-fol, Ri-fol, Tol-de-riddle-dee

although I wasn't too keen on the fol-de-rols.

Do you like butter?

How was it – when was it – someone started testing 'do you like butter?' by holding a buttercup under someone's chin and assessing the strength of the golden reflection? Modern children, with parents ever worried (understandably) about diet, somehow won't get the same pleasure from putting a buttercup under a friend's chin and asking 'Do you like low-in-cholesterol-high-in-polyunsatuarated-fats-butter-substitute?' – doesn't have the same ring, somehow.

The buttercup test

Requirements
1. One carefully picked buttercup.
2. Someone else's chin.

Method
1. The someone else lifts their chin.
2. You hold the buttercup underneath their chin.
3. You assess the degree of golden glow on their chin.
4. You pronounce them lovers of butter, or not.

Lucky clover

For some reason the time for me to look for a four-leaved clover was in the sixth form at school. We'd lounge around on the field in the sun in free periods or at lunchtime and as we sleepily gossiped, my fingers would part the leaves of the tight little clover plants looking for a four-leaved luck-charm. I don't think I ever found one although I'd sometimes 'manufacture' one to tease my friends. An Irish shamrock, it seems, has deep meaning for that faith-embracing nation: three leaves represent the Holy Trinity, with a fourth representing God's grace. For us, though, it was just good luck for passing the next exam or finding the right boy-friend – hoping we'd get the luck of the Irish.

I didn't grow up in the country, apart from patches of time at safe rural lettings during the war found for my mother, my sisters and me by my father, who had to stay in London throughout, so our free gifts and games from the natural world around us came from gardens and parks, and local over-grown derelict sites.

On the whole, during the sections of my childhood spent at our real home in Kent, I played in the street. I was the only girl in a rag-tail of boys: we skated and snow-balled, kicked balls and played cricket, rode bikes and invented secret clubs. I must have had some female company because many of the detailed, intricate creations from things found around us would have tried the patience of the rackety boys.

Grandmother, grandmother!
JUMP out of bed!

Another flower found everywhere – annoyingly in the garden, prettily in the hedge – was the convolvulus or bind weed. I was familiar with the white variety, an irritation to my father in the garden as it climbed towards the sun by twining (in a strictly clock-wise direction) round and round and throttling some innocent but prized flower or vegetable. I thought they were beautiful.

I didn't realise each flower lasted only a day since it would be stealthily succeeded by another identical bloom but I did destroy a fair few. We had a miniature game where we'd pick a white convolvulus flower and pinch it sharply on the green bracts at the base of the flower and watched the white flower head pop off for quite a distance, while chanting:

Grandmother, grandmother! JUMP out of bed!

for some strange reason – perhaps the white bell-like flower resembled an old lady's nightdress. It was only later I learned of the interesting pictures supplied by the seeds of the blue version of the convolvulus, morning glory…

Poppy doll

Children so often create people or the artefacts people use. I would be out to make a doll. I would carefully bend down the brilliant, poppy petals one by one until they touched the stem, gently so that they didn't become detached. I would have ready a long, flexible stem of grass which I would wind round at 'waist' high, creating a Marilyn Monroe hour-glass dress, tucking the ends of the grass in or even tying them if they were flexible enough. The coronet of black stamens on top of the green bulge of the ovary case looked like a curly, if slightly punk-ish, hairstyle. On the smooth shiny surface below I would scratch a face, using a thorn or a twig or anything else sharp I could find. To complete the illusion, the thick stem below the 'dress' would be split in two to make (rather hairy) legs – and I had a doll! I don't think I ever played with them, being more of a tom-boy than a little mother, but I loved making them. I never found out if my parents missed the poppies or even knew I was using them. In those days children spent hours outside, wandering around in their own realm of imagination and make-believe, or in the collective secret world of other children.

We had a long, thin garden behind our three-up, two-down semi. My parents were happy gardeners, their flowerbeds providing delightful illicit gifts. There was a patch of glorious, huge, flaming oriental poppies down on the left next to the fence. With the insouciant disregard of a child, I would pick at least one of these beauties, perhaps more if I made a mistake or became dissatisfied with the quality or size of the specimen, wholly thoughtless of the loving care of their cultivation.

How to make a poppy doll

1. With permission from whoever does the garden, pick one oriental poppy (those huge scarlet ones), keeping about 20cms (nine inches) of stem (Fig 1).
2. Very carefully bend down each petal to touch the stem.
3. With cotton or grass, bind the petals in the middle to the stem to form a 'waist', creating a dress (Fig 2).
4. Push another length of stem through at 'shoulder' level to create arms (Fig 3).
5. Draw a face on the green seed pod under 'hair' created by stamens (Fig 4).
6. Split stem to create legs (Fig 5).

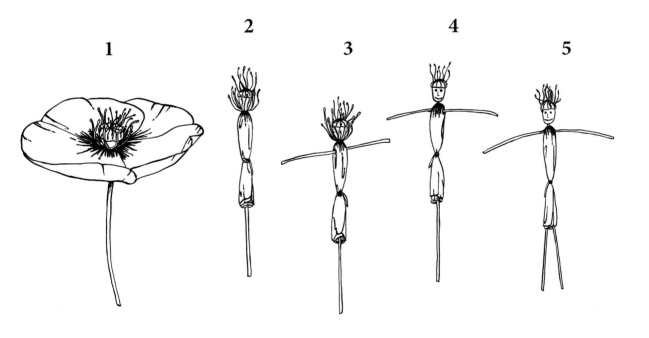

1   2   3   4   5

How to open the Californian poppy

The Californian poppy *eschscholtzia* gave me moments of quiet, secret pleasure. I certainly never learned early on how to spell it – apparently named after one Johann Friedrich von Eschscholtz, who must have had awful trouble with his name at school. I remember the flowers as a lovely deep, satisfying yellow, growing close to the ground where I could easily touch them when small.

There were many flowers in bloom at once, it seemed, and you had to search carefully for the prize – the green cap over a not-quite-opened one – which could be gently and satisfactorily pulled off, not damaging anything, giving the feeling you were freeing the luscious petals a tiny bit early to expand and open from their crumpled state. This was a very private, solitary action on my part – I wonder if other children discovered this miniature pleasure?

I still look for the caps, apparently fused sepals, even now when I see these delightful, hideously named flowers.

Fairy rings

Young children are fascinated by fairies, and sometimes the not-so-young are too. I think there's a deep longing that such beautiful other-worldly tiny creatures do exist and can be glimpsed or watched if only you're quick. So fairy rings appearing in early summer have an audience ready to marvel and admire. I remember seeing fairy rings in a field or on wasteland, and willing them to have been caused by fairies dancing round though the night, wearing out the grass.

When the mushrooms came up round the circle it seemed even more likely, with the image fixed in our minds of an elf sitting on one. I learned later of the folklore that said toads sat on them as well, giving rise to toadstools. Fairy rings maintain their magic, I think, even when you know they are caused by the dispersed spore of some energetic fungus.

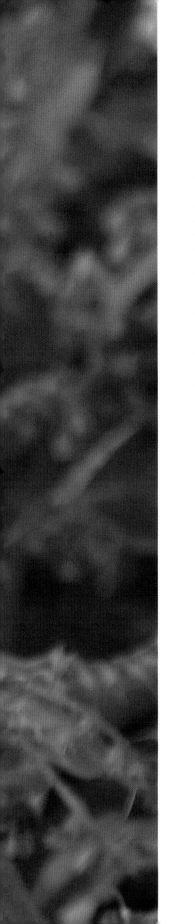

Foxglove thimbles

In the garden there were always snapdragons, or antirrhinums (another of those bizarrely spelt names like eschscholtzia) to play with, even without picking them. If you squeeze the base of the flower carefully, it will pop open and shut like the mouth of a dragon.

We also popped the flowers of foxgloves (*Digitalis purpurea*); an intriguing, beautiful plant in the wild or in people's gardens, it is poisonous, yet yields that useful heart drug *digitalis*. The *digitalis* part of its Latin name means thimble, while the foxglove bit may come from folk's glove, meaning the fairy folk and their gloves, all responding to its purple tubular bells.

Mind you, they look a bit big for fairy gloves, to me.

How to make a miniature garden

With time to spare in the long summer, a more detailed effort like a miniature garden became an attractive prospect. Children love things on their small scale and in their control, personal and private. Parents often allot their children patches of real garden to grow things in (why always carrots?), which is lovely but slow; a miniature garden looks good within the hour.

There are two main types of miniature garden – temporary and more permanent. In the former, any bits of plants or flowers can be stuck into the earth of the basic format for a pretty effect but of course they will die; if you want to go on admiring and tending the garden, the flowers must be real, small plants with roots which can be watered.

Whichever type you choose, it is such fun to create a tiny world, using earth or compost on a tray or baking tin as a base, with small rocks or stones, a mirror pond or a baking foil stream, a little house, a bridge, tiny flowering plants and twig trees. The possibilities are endless; indeed, a temporary miniature garden can be made in the wild, among the roots under a tree or on a rock, using whatever is to hand.

Miniature garden

Requirements

1. Old roasting tin, large plant pot 'saucer', shallow basket (lined) or any suitable container
2. Earth, potting/bulb compost
3. One or two smallish rocks or stones
4. Pocket mirror, tin foil, tin lid – anything to make pond and/or stream
5. Twigs, small artefacts, toys etc as wished
6. Pieces of moss if available

Method

1. If deep receptacle, cover bottom with thin layer of gravel/sand/pebbles for drainage
2. Cover with layer of soil/compost, made interesting by the creation of small mounds etc
3. Design your garden with pond, stream, paths, flower beds etc
4. Use moss to create 'lawns'
5. Place small plants appropriately
6. Use twigs etc to create trees, any other artefacts for special effects, such as bridge over stream, rocks etc
7. If gently watered – misted, not water-logged – garden should last for a while

NATURE'S WHISTLES

Wandering around in the peace was a good time to shatter it – using a whistle made from a blade of grass! This technique is passed down from child to child, or even granny to child in my case.

Grass whistle

I learned very early to make a hideously piercing noise by placing a flat grass blade carefully between my thumbs, creating tension as tightly as possible, and blowing through it. Of course the tighter I could hold it the higher-pitched the noise; it was also possible to make a satisfyingly rude noise by having the grass quite slack and vibrating loosely. The tighter/tauter the grass, the higher the note produced.

1. Pick a long, flat grass blade, at least 6 inches long.

2. Stretch it between your two side-by-side thumbs, trapped tautly between thumb joints.

3. With mouth touching thumbs, blow through them where curves create a small gap.

The squealing noise you ought to be able to make can apparently attract wild animals but we don't really have any of the large and frightening kind; in England it's more likely to attract the annoyance of any adult within earshot, which makes it fun. An even more sophisticated method uses two blades of grass but is the same otherwise.

A bright green new grass blade could be carefully 'pulled' from its sheath of larger blades: the revealed soft last few inches were succulent and tasty, especially on a hot, dusty summer's day.

Acorn whistle

A friend told me he could make an excellent noise using an acorn cup instead of grass, holding it between thumbs and forefingers, hollow towards the mouth, and blowing – but I confess I have never tried.

Owl hoots

1. With two thumbs side-by-side as in grass whistler, create as large a hollow space as you can by curving your hands, hands touching each other only with tips of fingers
2. Place mouth over first joined knuckles below thumb nails and blow
3. With practice, different notes can be created by altering size/shape of hollow space, once initial note is established – possible to play scale or tunes!
This noise can be so convincing that it even fools real owls who will reply by hooting back at you!

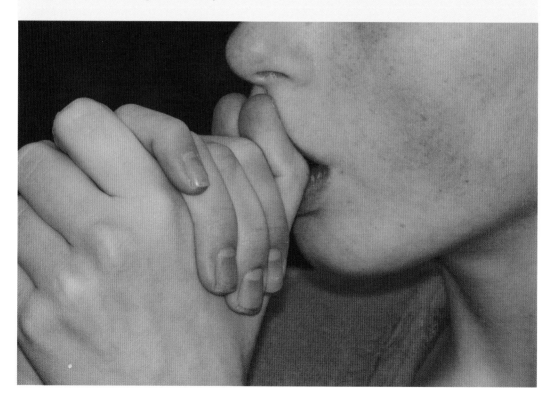

Fake grasshopper

Take a comb and stroke it down the edge of a piece of cardboard, and you have approximated the familiar chirping noise a grasshopper – but only a male – makes by rubbing its wings together in a peculiar and particular way, called 'stridulating'. They catapult themselves forward on long hind legs and can be used for grasshopper jumping contests if you are very careful not to harm them.

Nature close-up

A sweet-smelling hay meadow in the warm sun – what a wondrous place to lie and dream! As a child I loved putting my face close to the ground and watching the miniature world, with tiny, tiny flowers I could never name, ants and other small insects scurrying around and sometimes even that fascinating little creature, the grasshopper.

A friend has described to me how when she was a small child a large area of grassland nearby was mown for hay. She and her girl friends used to gather the mown grass up carefully (I can just imagine the glorious smell!) and shape small 'walls' into the ground plan of a house where they would 'play house' in all the various 'rooms' for hours, or until the boys came to kick it all down.

ROSE GAMES

Pot pourri

Summer flowers, especially blousy, full-blown roses, make many little girls (sorry to be sexist) think of using the pretty scented petals for something special, maybe for mum or gran. An easy one is an instant pot-pourri. If you can find a pretty bowl or box, just carefully pick as many scented petals as you can and mix them in the bowl. The perfume won't last long but it's the thought that counts! (Commercial pot-pourris have all sorts of chemical and artificial additives.)

Rose water

A more ambitious project is to make rose-water. Many of us have probably been disappointed that we've created something that soon goes 'off' and smells horrid by just pounding flower petals into water and assuming the resultant liquid is 'perfume'!

You may need help with this since to do it properly you will need access to a stove. Petals gathered, ideally, from a few different rose bushes, need to be placed into a saucepan of water and heated gently, but not boiled. The petals should turn transparent. When the liquid has been strained off, wait till it cools then keep it in the fridge, preferably in a pretty bottle or spray. It should smell nice for a while at least!

Potions and spells

Flower petals and strongly smelling leaves call out for being made into love potions and for use in magic spells. If you use the rose water method at least the concoctions will be reasonably wholesome – but don't drink any of them!

The Language of Flowers

Flowers have always been potent and expressive gifts, with a whole Victorian 'language of the flowers' to learn or use if you are so inclined.

- Snowdrop = hope
- Buttercup = wealth
- Forget-me-not = true love
- Lavender = mistrust
- White lily = purity
- Ox-eye diasy = patience
- Violet = faithfulness

Summer time, if you live in or near the countryside, is a time for wandering along the edge of cornfields or loitering in hay meadows. I was always taught to avoid damage – not to leave gates open, or spoil crops by treading them down. During one of the rural patches of my childhood, I can remember the exquisite joy of discovering the tiny flowers, scarlet pimpernel and germander speedwell, flourishing in the soil at the base of ripening wheat or oats. The brilliant blue of the speedwell with its white 'eye' contrasted with the even tinier pimpernel. Scarlet pimpernel flowers are open only when the sun shines; their habit of closing in dull weather has given the plant the name 'poor man's weather-glass.'

Fighting soldiers

Not everyone knows this: in summer, plantains provide a reasonably adequate pre-figuring of the delights of conker fights! Ribwort plantain grows everywhere, a common and hardy roadside plant, with tall tough stems culminating in dark flower heads.

Pick a strong-looking stem and challenge your friend to a battle. Simpler than conkers, knocking you opponent's head off, as it were, wins. One person holds the plantain upright, and the other just whacks with his own plantain: take it in turns, one whack each, until one of the heads flies off and the beheader has won.

An even more basic way to annoy someone is to wrap the stem of your plantain round its own head, pull it sharply and ping the head off directly at them.

Plantain pitched battles

You will need
Plantain heads with long stalks
An opponent

Process
1. A holds the plantain near the end of the stem, straight up in the air.
2. B holds his/her plantain about half way along and hits A's, trying to behead it. The beheader wins.

As a variation, the stem of the plantain can be bent round its own head which can then be satisfactorily pinged off at anyone.

AUTUMN

Chestnut tree at conker
time. Beware of its brittle
branches!

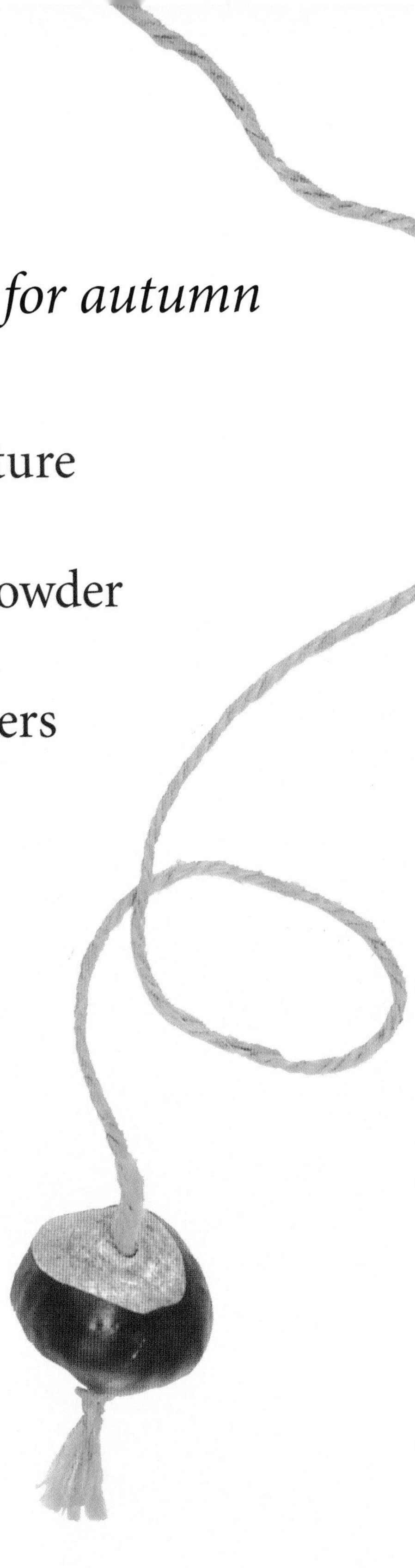

Some ideas for autumn

- Conker warfare
- Dolls' house furniture
- Conker knitting
- Rose hip itching powder
- Pine cone owls
- Sycamore helicopters
- Grass mats
- Will our love last?
- Bidibid burrs
- Flea darts
- Here's the bride
- Acorn cups
- Treasure troves
- Nature's larder
- Walnut cradles
- Elder pea-shooter

I think a child's year starts with autumn – back to school, perhaps a new school or a new class or a new teacher, back to school friends often at least a partially different set from the neighbourhood companions of the long summer, then it's the big build-up to Christmas. In the western adult world the natural new year starts with spring, although we're stuck with New Year's Day smack in the middle of winter.

Autumn was a magical time; we could play out until dusk and beyond. It was often still warm enough but weather was more exciting than in

summer, with wind and rain and scurrying leaves. There was school to go back to, friends to see again and holiday tales to swap.

I walked to my primary school in Kent – up my road, along the small main road, down the road parallel to mine, and along a road parallel to the main road – I can see every inch of the way now. In 'top juniors' I was allowed, (amazingly, looking back) to go to school on roller skates but for years I just happily meandered that familiar route alone.

I was intimately involved with every hedge and wall, knew where there'd be blossom trees in spring and conker trees in autumn.

Many of the hedges were privet, then as now. I would look earnestly for that massive magnificent moth, the privet hawk, but would only see its huge caterpillar in its green and purple splendour.

Fairy cobweb mirrors

Often in autumn (I don't know why autumn) I would pick a long thin green flexible twig from an unsuspecting hedge, strip its leaves and offshoots and bend it into a hoop.

Still, of course, wandering to or from school, I would then search the privet hedges for cobwebs, which I would 'collect' with the self-styled wand, turning it, in my eyes anyway, into a fairy cobweb mirror, which no self-respecting fairy could have used to see her beautiful reflection, of course, so what was all that about? I have never forgotten the sight, feeling and smell of those tiny 'mirrors', and they certainly helped my journey along.

Skeleton leaves

A child can touch and smell a leaf, inspecting its shape and structure. One friend told me she and her mates would pick one from a tree like broad-leaved lime and very carefully and slowly tear out the green of the leaf until they had a perfect skeleton – which they triumphantly called a fish bone.

I remember the enchantment of finding a naturally-decayed true leaf skeleton under a hedge or beneath a tree and marvelling at its spider-web delicacy and exquisite tracery – and I never knew what to do with it next. Perhaps I could have mounted it or used it for a dried flower picture but somehow I usually just put it back where I found it, as something too precious for heavy-fingered human activity.

KING CONKER

In autumn there were real treasures to look for, with the conker the undisputed leader. Horse chestnut trees are large, spreading and majestic – not easily missed – with leaves like rusty hands lying round as the year turned. Odd word, conker – perhaps from the word conqueror?

Each gang of kids knew where their best local conker trees were: dominating the school playground, overhanging the pavement from someone's garden, in a field, in the park. Ours was in the small copse at the end of our close. Suddenly everyone was collecting conkers, when the day before there wasn't one to be seen. Each year the gleaming mahogany surface was shinier than ever, so smooth to the fingers or against the lips.

We couldn't help running for the first one, then the next and the next, excited every year by their perfect beauty as they gleamed through a slit in the green prickly case. It was more unusual for a horse chestnut to fall still fully enclosed in its green, spiky jacket so it was especially prized.

We used to pull apart the case, exposing a perfect object no one else had ever seen or touched – it was ours in a very special way. Strangely, we were disappointed if there were twin nuts inside. Although pretty as they nestled their shapes round each other, and rare, they were too small for our purposes. I pick up conkers now, to feel again the silky skin, polished and perfect, with the rough, light-coloured scar.

We collected them – in pockets and bags and satchels and bike baskets. We didn't need them all but we wanted them all. They were free, beautiful and ours. We girls frowned on the rough boys who flung sticks and stones up into the branches to bring down more conkers, perhaps conscious that they could damage the branches, but we scrambled after the illicit booty nevertheless.

Conker warfare

At home began the serious preparation for conker warfare: should it be vinegar this year or should we beg mum for use of the oven? First, though, I needed to make holes in the few carefully chosen to be champions.

My mum always had a skewer or two in the kitchen drawer and they were the best, although a very long nail and a hammer were reasonable substitutes. The skewer needed to be carefully held in the flame of a gas ring until its last couple of inches were red hot – an excitingly dangerous exploit.

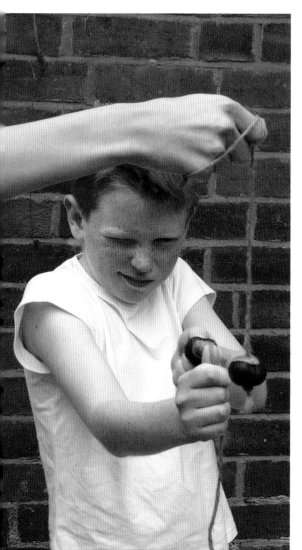

Pushing it down through the scar and then the flesh of a good big conker, while still red hot, took strength and precision – the displaced whitish kernel oozed out of the new hole and there was a distinctive smell. If you had to use a large nail it was always difficult to pull out again, the pulp clinging fast.

Most years I baked the conkers for a while in the oven, if allowed, or just took them to school as they were. Vinegar wasn't my choice for some reason. How long in the oven? How long did people soak them in vinegar? Who knows – each to his/her own secret theory. Now for the string: I always had fairly tatty bits of reclaimed string, so I had to use the skewer to push it through, and it always frayed. Lucky those who had a good, long shoe lace, with the metal tag making it easy to slot through the hole! However, I persevered, and lovingly tied a huge stopper of piled-on knots to form a plug – it was an awful defeat if your conker just slipped off its string during hostilities.

Preparing conkers for battle

1. Collect good-sized conker, removing green prickly outer casing
2. With scar upwards, carefully make hole downwards using a skewer (Fig 1), large nail or, for real perfection, Dad's wood drill (Fig 2)
3. Harden conker if required by baking briefly in low oven or soaking/ boiling in vinegar (adult help acceptable)
4. Poke length of string about 50cms (20 inches) or long shoelace down through hole using skewer or nail (Fig 3)
5. Tie large number of knots in underside end of string or shoelace to form large plug (Fig 4), making sure conker couldn't possibly slip off when whacked by opponent's conker (Fig 5)

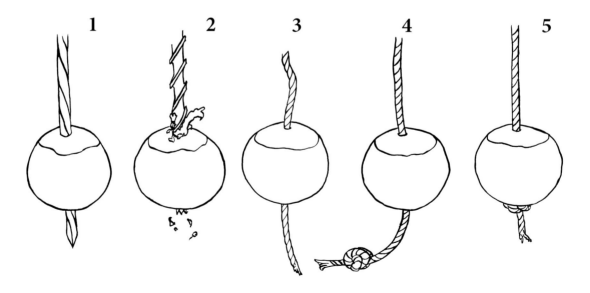

There were conker fights going on everywhere – in the playground, on the way to and from school, in the park – often with excited onlookers waiting to challenge the winner.

Conker rules

Rules were made up at will and argued over – what happens if the strings tangle? Was it deliberate? Did your opponent jerk their conker up just a little on purpose to spoil your aim? Occasionally my best conker would become a 1-er, a 2-er or a 3-er, depending on how many enemy conkers mine smashed but rarely did I manage anything grander.

It was very satisfying to splatter an opponent's champion by a great whack. Of course the boys swaggered around with mythical 20-ers and boasted of secret preparation but it was all in good spirit and nobody minded. Then, as suddenly as the craze started, conkers were old hat and disappeared.

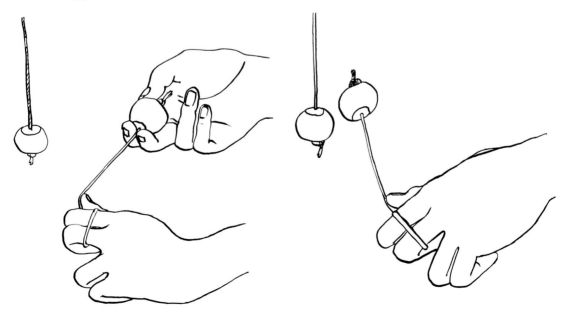

Dolls' house furniture

Girls took full competitive part in the conker battles but we had another use for those delectable objects. Probably because I was tall for my age, I always took a great delight in miniature things: the polished mahogany of conkers said *dolls' furniture* to me and to some of my friends.

We'd beg and borrow nails or tacks and a hammer from our dads, or in my case, just use (with permission) whatever was needed from my father's shed down the garden.

A flat-ish conker, with four nails knocked in underneath, became a table. Add two nails on top and wind wool round to form the back and I had a chair; further elaboration and I could create an armchair or a cradle.

1 **2**

You couldn't make much else, and they were fairly unsatisfactory because they were knobbly and lost their shine after a while but I loved making them, always expecting them to be perfect.

To make dolls' furniture from conkers

1. Find some thin, flat conkers – often two together in casing.
2. Table – four small nails or tacks knocked in underneath to form legs. Acorns can be the cups (Fig 1).
3. Chair – same as 2, then add two more tacks on top to form chair back (Fig 2). Make back more comfortable by winding wool round the two tacks (Fig 3).
4. Armchair – as 2 and 3, then add two smaller tacks (or bang them in further) to form arms. Wind wool round back and arms (Fig 4).

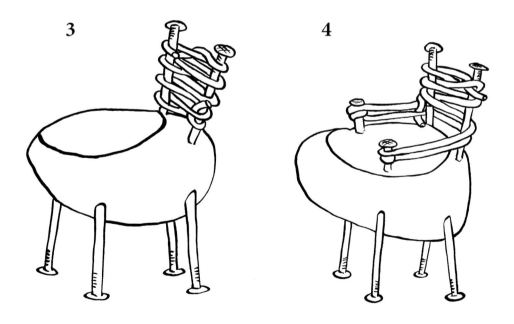

3

4

Conker knitting

Conkers had another use for those fiddly, industrious fingers of little girls. If you couldn't lay your hands on one of the then-current but now rare wooden cotton reels – how inferior are today's hollow plastic apologies – a good thick conker would work for a while. French knitting or knitting nancy! The little balls of brightly coloured wool remnants begged from grandma or found at the bottom of someone's sewing box were gleefully collected, with the conker, four nails, a hammer, a skewer and a Kirby grip. (Don't know what they are? You can still buy them – bent double, flat wavy metal strips with blobbed ends for safety, ranked meticulously across cardboard, a cheap and 'invisible' way to curb unruly curls.)

As large a hole as possible, without splitting it, would be skewered through the conker and the four nails would be carefully knocked in equidistantly round the hole. To start the 'knitting', an end from one of the balls of wool would be wrapped round the base of a nail, with the final last few coloured inches pushed down through the hole. Wrapping the long length of wool twice round the outside of the ring of nails would create a loop which, with the Kirby grip, could be lifted over the head of a nail, and then on to the next, round and round the circle. The tail of wool, dangling outside at the base, could be pulled downwards as that magic coloured snake of tubular 'knitting' emerged longer and longer – if your patience allowed you to go on round and round, lifting the loops over the nail heads. How you looked forward to the second colour, tied on as the first ran out, and then the third and fourth, emerging in squared perfection as you gently pulled!

The finished colourful snake was ready now to be spiralled into a flat circle, sewn in place and presented proudly to a long-suffering, oh-so-grateful mother, as a splendid, garish table-mat she would have on indulgent display for at least a week or two before it got 'lost in the wash' or 'given to Mrs Along-the-Road because she admired it so much'.

French knitting using conkers

1. Find large, 'tall' conker
2. Make hole down through middle as if preparing for a conker battle, but make the hole wider
3. Knock four tacks or small nails into top of conker round hole
4. Push one end of coloured wool down through hole, leaving tail dangling (Fig 1)
5. Tie same coloured wool to one tack
6. Wind wool round the outside of all four tacks twice (Fig 2)
(continued next page)

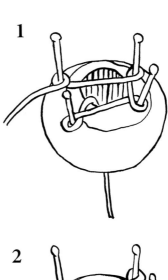

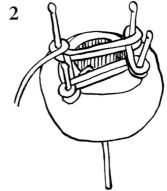

7. Using hairgrip or bodkin (blunt-ended needle) lift one loop over tack (Fig 3)

8. Continue round and round, winding wool round circle of tacks and lifting loops over each tack in turn (Fig 4)

9. Pull tail down at regular intervals as you knit, changing wool colour as often as wanted by tying on new colour before winding round tacks.

10. Completed coloured 'snake' can be sewn in flat circle to create table mat.

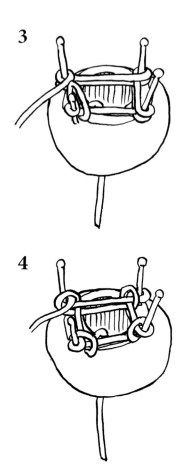

PINE CONES

Pine cones - odd, mysterious autumn treasures. I have always loved finding them, all brown and knobbly, big and small, tall and thin or short and fat, green or brown, fanned open or tightly furled. They name their own trees - conifers if bearing cones. The brown female cone is the one we notice, the scaly seed cases arranged in swirls, like the whorls on a sea shell, that make you think you could solve the mathematical secrets of the universe by studying them. They burn beautifully on open fires and can be silvered or painted for Christmas decorations.

Pine cone owls

You will need
A full, fat-ish pine cone. If it is too tightly closed,
warm it on a radiator, for example, to open it up.
Either paper or felt for eyes, ears and beak.
If wanted, a twig or log to glue the owl on.
Glue.

Process
1. Make sure the cone will be able to 'perch', pointed side up, by either
removing some seeds from the bottom or sand-papering it flat.
2. Cut a beak from paper or felt and stick on.
3. Stick on big eyes – the wiggly ones you can buy are lovely but paper
ones are fine.
4. Cut a beak from paper or felt and stick on. The owl can either be glued
to the twig or hung up.
5. A 'family' of different sized cones look lovely.

1   **2**   **3**   **4**

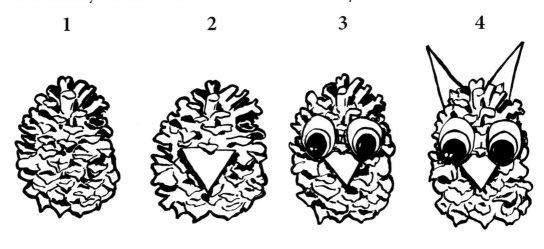

Boys plague the girls

Crane flies (daddy-long-legs) were often around on warm, moist September days.

A friend described to me how boys at her school used to catch live crane flies and put them into their mouths, walk up to a girl, open their mouths wide and huff the live cranefly into the girl's face – definitely a do-not-do-this-at-home activity, not least because the crane fly could easily lose one of their loosely-jointed dangly legs in the process. Are children kinder to animals today?

Their larvae, the notorious leather-jackets, so called because of their dark brown shiny skin, eat away at vital roots under the surface of the precious turf of a lawn or a park, so they are not very popular. If you find them they wiggle unpleasantly so they are not very attractive, either.

Scrumping for apples

Another autumnal activity, I believe sometimes secretly carried out by my momentarily (I hope) wayward children, was scrumping. As everyone

knows, this is nicking apples from a neighbour's tree when they aren't looking. There's something traditional about it which almost makes it acceptable, as long as no harm is done to the trees of course, but I couldn't possibly recommend it…

In our long thin Kent garden we had a cooking apple tree (too sour), an eating apple (not bad) and two pear trees – one absolutely delicious if you had the patience to wait for the fruit to ripen properly, the other like turnips. Eating a ripe pear, juice dripping down your arm, reading a book in the autumn sunshine, must be one of life's glories.

Autumn leaves

Autumn gave us children the exhilarating pleasure of scrunching through drifts of crisp brown fallen leaves, kicking them up and throwing them around and over each other, making a legitimate, un-punishable MESS! A simple competition was to see who could catch the most leaves with one hand before they hit the ground, within a stated time. On a quieter level, finding the most beautiful colours – red, orange, yellow and still some green – on a single fallen leaf, marvelling at the bright magic from nowhere, perhaps putting it in the leaves of a book or carefully drawing its particular shape and colouring it in.

Grass or reed mats

If you have a reed bed or some rushes nearby, it is fun to make square table mats by weaving the long stems in and out. I did try, clumsily, to make small table mats from reeds but they were never very successful although I enjoyed trying. Having found appropriate reeds or even tall, strong-stemmed grass, we would collect enough to start. It was always encouraging to find two different shades of green or golden brown for the warp and the weft but that wasn't essential.

I had never learned to weave but the basic system of under-and-over worked. We'd try to start with a few same-length stalks lying the same way on the ground and call them the warp, then we'd weave in another, differently shaded if possible, going across, over and under each warp stem, for the weft – we enjoyed the names if nothing else. It was possible to create a slightly wonky square of interwoven stems with a lovely pattern which could be proudly presented at home as a table mat but it usually wobbled-off any plate or cup placed upon it.

Instructions for grass/reed table mats

You will need
1. A bundle of reeds, rushes or long strong grass stems of roughly the same length, depending how large your table mat is to be
2. A knife or scissors to cut the stems
3. Lots of patience and a nice sunny day or a warm fire-side

Process
1. Cut some of whichever stems you have to the required length – you will not necessarily know how many you will need
2. Lay a few, six or seven, stems side-by-side on the ground
3. A few inches in from one edge, weave a stem through the stems on the ground without dislodging them, carefully going over one then under the next, over one and under the next, until you are at the other side
4. The second stem you will need to weave in the alternate manner – ie under then over, under then over. You will need to push it carefully right up next to the first stem
5. Continue with alternating over and under, under and over, until you have completed the square, each time pushing the new stem next to the one before to create a tight weave and a regular pattern

SEED DISPERSAL

Trees and plants in autumn were all frantically preserving their genes, although I didn't realise this was the reason for the fruits and nuts, the clever or sometimes bizarre mechanisms of seed dispersal.

The proud parent tree or plant can use the wind or a creature's digestive processes or the heat of the sun to spread its precious seed, or it can make use of passing animals, including human ones – sticking its seed on to fur, wool or clothes because sooner or later the host will get rid of it, further down the line.

Seed dispersal, the urgent desire for plants to reproduce their species, has always created special delight for children.

Sycamore helicopters

Whirligigs, helicopters – the joys of sycamore keys! Whirling like liberated propellers un-summoned from the sky, in slow measured arabesques, they spin straight into children's hearts and games. I remember just watching them, or tossing them back up to the sky just to watch again. But others had variations on this simple pleasure: who could throw one the highest? Whose whirligig would spin the most number of times before hitting the ground? Whose hit the ground first in a straight race when thrown from the same height? I even heard you could split them in half, sticking one wing on your nose... A very successful method

of propagation – sycamores spring up everywhere, wanted or not, their maple-like leaf an elegant shape to come across fallen on the path.

Ash keys

Keys to children unlock things: a bunch of green keys from the ash tree can be hung on a gaoler's belt in an exciting game of cops and robbers.

On my own in woodland, dazed and enchanted by the uncanny mystery and beauty – the silence was scary because strange noises could happen at any moment – I remember wishing and wishing the single ash key in my hand could unlock a secret door in the bark of an old, twisted tree? In a moss-covered rock? I had heard or read stories of such things and it seemed to be possible that an ash key could open a different world, a different universe. It never did but I didn't stop hoping.

Ash trees have been thought of as magic in many cultures, so perhaps I wasn't far wrong. Apparently in Norse mythology the first man, Ask, was formed from an ash tree; in Ireland the shadow from an ash tree was said to damage crops. Its leaves, bark and keys were thought to cure otherwise incurable ailments before modern medicine took over.

> *Ashen tree, ashen tree,*
> *Pray buy these warts off me.*

or give an advanced weather forecast:

> *Oak before ash, in for a splash*
> *Ash before oak, in for a soak*

Acorn cups

Acorn cups found in woodland have always fascinated by their tiny perfection and adaptability. The acorn snugly in its cup, depicted in a simple stencil, is an evocative image on fingerposts to indicate long distance walks.

An acorn can be slipped out so neatly, a hard, perfect shape but what to do with it? Most children have surely played tea-parties with the cups, although for them to stand upright they need to be rasped against a stone on the bottom to create a reasonably flat base.

They invoke fanciful other-worldly uses – Charles Lamb, in his tale of *A Midsummer Night's Dream*, describes the behaviour of their tiny subjects when Queen Titania and King Oberon quarrel:

> *'till all their fairy elves would creep into acorn-cups and hide themselves for fear.* – Charles Lamb

They are a fairy device, so beautifully made. A child with an acorn cup can wonder and imagine. Even adults have taken these tiny scraps of hard, curved wood and carved miniature artefacts from them.

I still can't resist picking up acorns, pushing out the nuts – and I look in wonder, still, at the perfect cups.

Will our love last?

It is an old Welsh custom for young girls to take two acorn cups and name one for their boyfriend and one for themselves; the acorn cups are floated in a bowl of water and if the acorn cups sail together, they will get married but if they drifted apart, their relationship would not last.

Will our love last? (Part 2)

Another 'love test' is actually a lesson in science. I heard recently of this sophisticated stratagem. A small piece of paper would have cut into it the current fancied-one's name or initials, then using little paper clips this would be delicately fastened onto the flat of a large leaf still growing on a tree or bush and left for some hours of bright sunshine.

After removing the paper, it would be seen that photosynthesis had obediently written the beloved inscription onto the leaf for eternity – or at least until the leaf dropped in the autumn.

Bidibid burrs

More irritating and therefore more effective were the burrs from a roadside plant with the wonderful New Zealand Maori name of bidibid. We would find the burrs stuck to each other even when dry and dead-looking, and you would get small clusters of them on top of a stem which you could pull off, aware of how dry and prickly they were, brownish-yellow-dusty-red.

They could be thrown or surreptitiously placed on a companion's clothing or, much worse, onto their heads – very unkind, this, because they

Sticky seed dispersal

For us children, oh endless, innocent, harmless childish fun – stick something to your friend's, your brother's, your sister's back (behind their back) and run away laughing, or keep silent, hoping when it is discovered they'll be embarrassed. There are many perfect partners for this simple larking about.

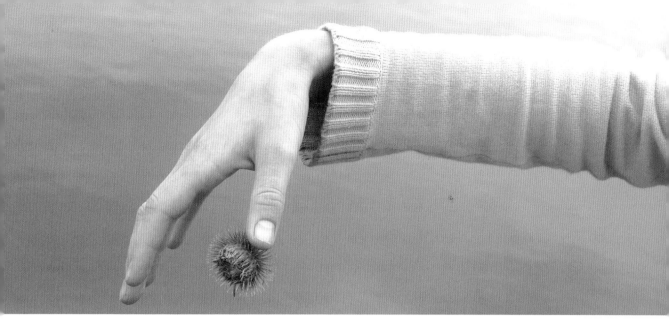

would be as difficult to remove from people's hair as chewing gum. Somehow I always managed to stick at least one burr inadvertently onto my own woollen clothing where it would disintegrate as I tried to pull it off, leaving small scratchy bits which would irritate through the wool for days afterwards.

Under a microscope the small hooks on the burrs can be seen – these apparently so inspired a Swedish engineer when he was a child, he later invented that useful modern marvel, velcro, on the same principle. I can see how he might; the burrs are lethal.

Flea darts

My children called these next delights by the elegant name of flea darts: one type of grass has seeding arrangements which look like under-developed ears of barley and can be thrown like a javelin, with a wonderfully flighted path, to stick into someone's coat or jumper. We didn't give them such a descriptive identity as 'flea darts': I don't remember calling them anything special, but I can see that the grass heads which look as if they are full of black nits are well, if vulgarly, named.

They stick in like anything, hanging down from the hooked point so that if you pull them out carelessly, you are left with the tapeworm's head, as it were, which will itch invisibly through your clothes for days.

Of course the couch grass, burrs and flea darts were evolved to stick to passing animals but what pleasure they've given human children ever since, freely available, with no damage done! Damage to clothing could certainly be done by the mischievous pinging of elderberries at the bright white T-shirt of friend or enemy – as the berries sploshed, they dyed: an early example of nature's own paint-balling.

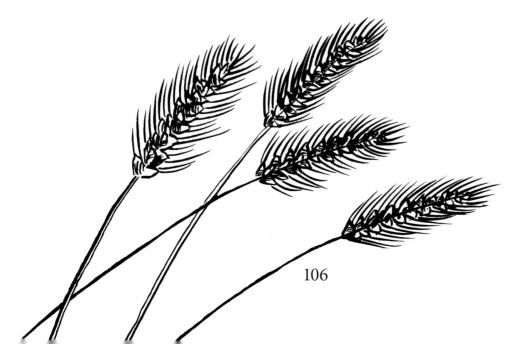

Stickywilly

Cleavers, Goosegrass, Stickywilly, Stickyweed, Catchweed, Coachweed – all wonderful names, perfect instruments for annoying your friends. You could pull long strands of its bright green streamers from wherever this ubiquitous plant had twined itself and it would stick to anything – jumpers, coats, hair, socks.

You could even make patterns on your own clothes with it, like green embroidery. After a cleavers battle the strands would all be pulled harmlessly off together with the round bobble seeds and discarded by the wayside – now far from the mother plant.

107

Rose hip itching powder

As a young child, living through the various upsets and confusions of WW2, my stable memories are of living mainly in our 1930s semi, in a child-friendly close where all the kids played out endlessly, in rain, shine or snow. It was a secret street life, intense and imaginative, with tricks and games, clubs and cloak-and-dagger signs and languages.

Our small front garden had a short brick wall topped by a dense hedge of briar rose. In autumn, the gloriously red rose hips were a convenient source of friend-annoyance ammunition.

I used to bite off or peel with my finger nails the red flesh, eating some of it, unwittingly increasing my vitamin C intake, and then I would carefully harvest into a paper bag or a grubby handkerchief the seeds inside, with their fine, hair-like filaments. These were clearly designed to spread the rose's DNA but we had other uses: carefully and clandestinely slipped inside the collar of an unsuspecting friend or enemy, they itched and itched efficiently for hours, causing much misery and fun.

Recipe for itching powder

1   Pick bright red rosehips from dog rose (briar or brier rose) bushes.
2   Carefully peel off red flesh – good for eating, full of vitamin C.
3   Each hip is full of seeds with very irritating hairs – collect all these carefully in a paper bag or envelope.
4   When friend isn't looking, put few hairy seeds down back in side collar.
5   Friend's back will itch for hours.

Here's the bride

My daughter and her friends had a delicate little trick with a stalk of quaking grass, broadcasting its seeds efficiently. Saying a short rhyme as they did the actions, in the space of a few seconds they created a wedding:

> *Here's the bride [holding up the flowering stem]*
> *In her pride*
> *Here's her bouquet*
>   *[squeezing up the florets into a bunch between finger and thumb]*
> *'I do' they say*
> *Here's the confetti*
>   *[pulling florets up off the stalk and tossing them in the air]*
> *Good luck, my pretty!*

Or a simpler version [with similar actions throughout]:

> *Summer tree*
> *Winter tree*
> *Bunch of flowers*
> *April showers*

Squirrelling away

Seed dispersal fascinated me, once I'd heard of it. I worked so enthusiastically on my Seed Dispersal Collection Project (see page 112), back now at home after evacuation and in primary school in Kent during the austere post-war period. I still think with pride of my laboriously-gathered display: it was great fun and very satisfying. I expect I had enormous help but, like all children, my peers were vividly in technicolour foreground, with parents, school teachers and siblings the permanent but sepia backdrop.

I had a white cardboard shoebox – or maybe two or more, because of the layers. I had the trays of old match boxes, I had cotton wool. Each carefully garnered seed, with its attendant wings or hooks or edible coverings, had its own carefully labelled match box tray, where it was advantageously displayed on cotton wool.

The Seed Dispersal Project

Equipment needed

2 shoeboxes with lids
Empty match boxes big and small, or equivalent small cardboard trays.
Cotton wool
Thin card to cut up for labels, pen
Collection of seeds, seed pods, nuts, seed heads, burrs, 'keys', berries, hips, haws etc

Method

1   Cover bottom of first shoe box with layer of variously-sized match box trays or other open, shallow container
2   Put thin layer of cotton wool in each container
3   Carefully place one specimen of seed dispersal in each container, displayed to best advantage
4   Write identification neatly on tiny piece of card laid next to specimen within container, identifying plant name and method of dispersal ie.　　Sycamore
　　　　　　　　　　　　　　　By wind
5   When bottom of first box is covered, create new layer by using inverted lid of second shoe box. Attach card strips, ribbon, string for handles to enable lid to be lifted off bottom layer safely
6   Fill second layer as first
7   Decorate final lid, including name of creator and date created.

The filled match box trays first covered the floor of the shoe box, then – and here I can't quite remember: did I have the lid of a second shoe box inserted to protect the first layer and to provide a home for the second layer? Did I have even a third layer, another shoe box lid? I know the lid of the original shoe box was triumphantly placed on top, and I can picture it full to the brim, with no doubt my name and the project's title carefully written on the clean, white cardboard surface.

I wonder what happened to it? I think it was admired at school but I expect I tired of it, as children do. It has left me, though, with indelibly retained 'facts' about how water and wind, animals and birds (and humans) assist trees and plants to survive and multiply.

Like growing mustard and cress on damp flannel, or grass 'heads' (grown in a peat-filled stocking) or watching the class tadpoles grow legs, lose their tails and turn into frogs, school nature study had a profound effect on me and doubtless on millions of other children.

Does it still happen today? Or has it, like conkers, (barmily, in my eyes) been banned from school playgrounds for reasons of Heath and Safety; has it given way to learning from the internet?

TREASURE TROVE

Children love to collect things. The collection is theirs, under their control, available for re-counting, closer scrutiny or smug showing off whenever it's needed. At one time I collected jugs – why? I'm not sure the family even noticed and I didn't reach double figures.

We used to buy sealed packs of wonderful cigarette cards (the nearest I came to smoking) at a special local shop when we had sufficient saved-up pocket money. Mine, of course, were usually the beautiful British wild flower sets. I sometimes had a craze for collecting and drying the flowers themselves, carefully picking just one with its leaves, where there were plenty.

I would arrange each specimen 'artistically' between sheets of pink blotting paper (not available nowadays for children, presumably) inside the pages of the thickest book I could find, with other weighty tomes piled on top – I never rose to the grand height of a proper wooden flower press. I can't remember I ever did anything with them after that, although I look with admiration on people's clever dried flower creations trapped in glass or forming intricate pictures. It is certainly a lovely way to make delightful cards for mum or grandma, if a child has patience and neat fingers – there will always be some appropriate flowers, leaves or grasses around somewhere.

When my children were young we did live in the country for a few years. On our long walks we sometimes came across tiny, fragile bones and skulls of birds that had died in the hedgerows. I think I even remember boiling the remains of a rabbit we found to free up its elegant skeleton for their collections.

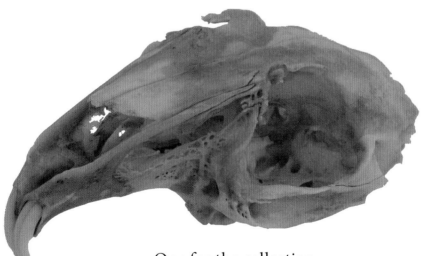

One for the collection:
a rabbit skull

Children collect coloured stones, stones with holes in, questionable arrow heads and dodgy fossils, feathers, sea shells and dead smelly star fish. Some families joined in the craze for polishing coloured stones and bought one of those special machines; I liked the idea but the end-products of clumsy rings and well-meaning bottom-heavy pendants were an anti-climax, and the stones much more attractive before all the fuss.

Some children collected live creatures, like Gerald Durrell, with ladybirds in matchboxes, snails in a drawer and tiddlers in a jar or live crabs in buckets but I preferred my collections to be static and arrange-able.

There is an unearthly, eldritch beauty about sea shells; it must be the perfection of their shape, colours and patterning. I can remember gazing at one of those tiny pink-washed shells that fit over the tip of a child's finger, agog at its flawless beauty.

It might have gone unseen by anyone if I hadn't picked it up by chance, so what was that all about?

If I had read Gray's *Elegy* by then I might have earnestly quoted to myself;

> *"Full many a flower is born to blush unseen and waste its sweetness on the desert air"*
> Thomas Gray

The seaside, which I think we visited rarely when I was little, is a place for observations and collections. At the right kind of seaside there were rock pools; if you knelt down and looked into them properly, concentrating and shutting out everything else, you could be part of a tiny, eerie world of strange mini-monsters and bizarre plants, waving around in their translucent world.

Predicting the weather with seaweed

We looked for seaweed to take home and hang outside to predict the weather – if the seaweed was wet, it was probably raining!

Popping bladder wrack

Or we found wonderful yellow-black slimy bladder wrack, covered in air-pockets like tiny cushions which apparently serve to keep it afloat and therefore near the light of the sun, but for us they were the natural popping equivalent of bubble-wrap, especially if the piece we found was dry and brown.

NATURE'S LARDER

Children are perennially hungry and there is a natural larder out there for their voracious, never-appeased appetites – as long they learn what is safe and what is not. Children today may have seen those hearty, bush-tucker-type programmes on television; our gentle lanes, hedges, fields and woodlands yield up a much more modest menu, like the woodland sorrel I learned to nibble during our war-time family walks, but there is plenty of variety, rolling with the seasons.

From the earliest months of their lives children put things in their mouths so it is sensible for them to know the free samples they can safely eat from nature's supermarket. They divide roughly into sections: berries, nuts and others.

Blackberries

Berries are colourful and succulent, enticing to animals, birds, insects and, of course, children. It is a common sight in autumn to see families with bags and baskets at the side of the road brambling, that is picking black-berries. Picked and eaten too early, before they plump up and turn that wonderful dark, dark purple, they are too tart and probably give tummy-aches to the greedy but eaten ripe straight off the bush, warmed by the evening sun, they are delicious! Of course they can be taken home and cooked with apples or made

118

A finger-tip search for bilberries

into jelly but their flavour is quite delicate and, in my view, best savoured straight from the hedgerow. They are a powerful dye, so watch out for your clothes!

Bilberries

I can't tell you in a personal sense about bilberries, except you could call them whinberries, whortleberries, whimberries, blaeberries and many other local names, and it is said they are delicious, especially made into jams, juices, jellies, medicines for the eyes and liqueurs – but I don't think I have ever tasted them. They grow on woody shrubs on moorland and heaths and almost anywhere if the soil isn't very good, it seems. The American equivalent, blueberries, must be very good for pies.

Wild strawberries

Wild strawberries – how romantic those words sound! They are such treasures to come across, smaller than their overblown cultivated descendants but much sweeter and tastier. There are different theories about the name strawberry – the word itself probably older than the custom of bedding the plants on straw, although apparently there was a tradition of collecting wild strawberries, threading them on straws and selling or giving them by the strawful. A likely explanation may be the sprawling habit of the wild plant, the runners appearing to have been strewn across the ground. Another old custom was that if you share a double wild strawberry with someone you may well fall in love with them – so beware!

Rose hips

Wild roses brighten up the autumn and winter hedgerows with their brilliant scarlet rosehips or haws. They are tedious to peel, the insides useful for itching powder (see page 109), but the flesh is quite tasty and packed full of vitamin C. Personally, apart from using their seeds to plague friends, I never found them worth the effort as snacks – better left for the birds, such as robin, blackbird, dunnock, green finch and many other hedgerow feeders. I remember a drink diluted, I think,

from Rose Hip Syrup during the war (it tasted faintly of metal, I recall, and not much else), taking its strengthening place next to that gorgeous delicacy cod-liver-oil-and-malt which always clung sensuously to the teaspoon needing very determined licking to garner the last smear.

Crabapples and others

Crabapples are too tart to eat on the move but could be taken home to add to various culinary delights. Sloes from blackthorn trees are so bitter they are really only good for making sloe gin or for use in helping to set other jams and jellies – they aren't really child-fodder, anyway.

Elder, with its flattened masses of creamy blossom, is endemic in the English countryside and invades many gardens. The flowers have an unpleasant smell, and the elderberries that follow in the autumn have an underlying matching nasty flavour but, if that doesn't put you off, they *are* edible. The ubiquity of the tree, with its pungent bark, blossoms and berries, has ensured its herbal, vinous and magical uses over the centuries. It has sometimes been accredited with evil powers and sometimes the opposite, like the knack of warding off the evil eye of witches.

The ease of using hollowed out elder twigs for making pipes and flutes has encouraged an association with Pan, the Ancient Greek God of pastures and herdsmen, music and hunting. This has been an important tree for Britain throughout the ages – but it still smells horrid.

Sucking nectar

Coming into the 'others' category, like wood sorrel – is nectar, the food of the gods. Although it will hardly appease stomach pangs, it is a tiny refreshment. As children we sucked nectar from honeysuckle, from dead nettle flowers, from clover – from any flower that seemed promising. We knew we could have dandelion leaves in a salad at home and could pick the circular nasturtium leaves from the garden to add a hot, peppery taste – even the vivid nasturtium flowers are similarly peppery and edible and wonderfully decorative, provided you wash off the voracious blackfly not hoovered up by a helpful ladybird.

NUTRITIOUS NUTS

Nuts are easy and a joy to collect. Autumn blesses us with these little beautifully-packaged snacks in her larder, tasty and good for most of us, unless we're burdened by a nut allergy.

Roasting sweet chestnuts

Sweet chestnuts, not to be confused with horse chestnuts or conkers which are not edible, can certainly be eaten straight from the tree but they are best, indeed delicious, roasted.

We were lucky enough to have an open fire when I was a child: sweet chestnuts were spread on an old all-metal coal shovel which was thrust into the glowing fire. The smell as they roasted! We would jiggle them from hand-to-hand, nibbling at the sweet, tender lobes of the kernel, enjoying the burnt bits and spitting out the bitter skin.

Sweet chestnut trees are not native to Britain, but were probably brought here by the Romans when they invaded us, so they are not as widespread as conker trees and are often found in parks or large gardens.

I can remember being able to collect sweet chestnuts in the wild only rarely as a child, so we had to persuade our mother to buy them from the greengrocer so that we could roast them cosily on a cold autumn evening. A child who is near enough to a sweet chestnut tree to collect these delicious morsels is lucky indeed. They are used in cooking, ground for flour or turned (commercially) into Christmas treats: chestnut stuffing, purée or marrons glacés.

Hedgerow hazelnuts

Hazelnuts or cobnuts are often found in the hedgerows since the hazel tree has been used for hedging and coppicing for centuries. The nuts are in clusters, with the bracts or leafy envelopes holding the nuts shorter than those of its cousin, the filbert. The shells of these small but tasty, nutritious nuts are very hard so watch your teeth! The kernel can be eaten straight out of the shell, if it's ripe, or roasted, added to chocolate or a myriad other uses. I've always seen hazelnuts as the bread-and-butter of our nut family, not glamorous or rare but a handful of them are friendly and companionable to have in the pocket for a quiet munch – if you've strong teeth or a stone handy to crack the shells.

Walnuts

Bigger and somehow more important are walnuts. They are easy to collect and full of nutritious goodness. They can be eaten raw, once you have learned the knack of cracking the shell along the 'joint' but, beware! – the juice of un-ripe walnuts will dye your fingers as if you're smoking 40 cigarettes a day, a dead give-away for clandestine walnut-pinching! Once out of the shell, especially if you can extract it whole, a walnut looks uncomfortably like the human brain; perhaps that's why one old tradition says they cure headaches, another that they cause headaches.

Walnuts are used in sweets, chocolates and all sorts of cooking but are fun to eat straight from the shell if you like the slightly (I think) oily taste. I remember tiny elaborate 'picks' at home for extracting pieces of walnuts (and brazil nuts, even more difficult) from the shell.

Walnut cradle

I think the most delightful use of a walnut half-shell, especially for a motherly little girl (or indeed a fatherly little boy) is a tiny cradle. It takes some ingenuity to create the dainty covers and pillow, and the baby, but it can be a thing of real beauty that a child could keep amongst those treasures of childhood we marvel at and are glad to see again as adults. It will be difficult to balance the walnut cradle on its ridged bottom so it could hang, and rock beautifully, from a thin ribbon either tied all round under the ex-joining rim with long loops each end, or glued on.

Walnut shell cradle

1. Remove all traces of nut from one half shell
2. Make tiny paper or material sheets and a pillow
3. Make a tiny doll – plasticine or paper – and place in cradle
4. Tie thin string or narrow ribbon round under the rim of the shell, dangle from something so that cradle rocks

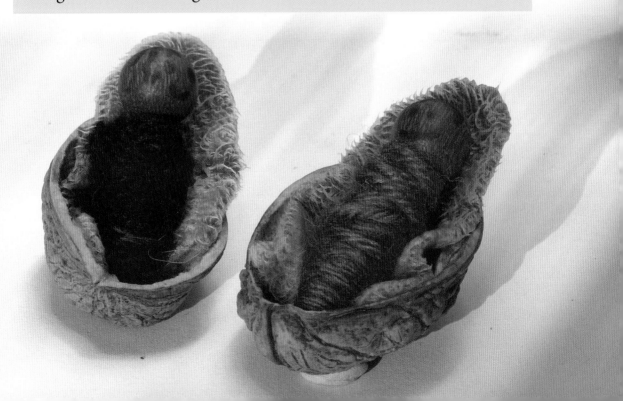

Walnut shell boats

A perfect half-shell can become a tiny boat, especially if you have or can make a crew small enough to sail in her. To fix a twig or match stick mast for a paper sail, a child could be helped to fill the hollow of the shell with melted candle wax or perhaps plasticine or play-doh would work.

Walnut shell boat

1. Separate two halves of walnut shell
2. Take one half and remove all kernel
3. Fill half shell with melted wax, plasticine, play doh or equivalent
4. Stick in twig/matchstick/toothpick/cocktail stick/drinking straw
5. Slot on leaf or paper sail

As an ancient and important tree, although not native to Britain, the walnut has its own clutch of myths and legends. One misogynistic rhyme says:

A spaniel, a woman, and a walnut tree
The more they're beaten, the better still they be.

although no-one seems to know its origin, apart from probably being Russian – thanks, comrades! Another perhaps more useful superstition says if a walnut is dropped onto the lap of a person suspected of being a witch, she will be unable to get up from her chair as long as the walnut stays there.

Walnut shell lockets

The empty walnut shell can be a source of endless joy to a child. If you can manage to keep the pair of half-shells hinged after extracting the 'meat', what a wonderful tiny secret hiding place this can be, or a natural locket for small photos, a possible gift for someone special.

CHILD WARRIORS

Perhaps we didn't collect feathers in the ordinary way of collating and identifying but we used them. Strange how children embrace mediaeval weapons of personal destruction with such gusto and inherited knowledge!

Sword-bearing knights

We found sturdy sticks, sharpened one end (on a stone if we hadn't a penknife between us), clumsily tied a short cross-piece on – and lo! we were sword-bearing knights, regardless of gender, skilled at sword-fighting and raring for chivalric deeds. I am amazed our eyes remained un-poked as we flailed around, our second hands elegantly in the air as we swash-buckled around like Stewart Granger or Errol Flynn. Of course without string and a cross-piece, we had an equally useful spear – but there's not much you can do safely with a spear so they became more a carried fashion statement.

Just sitting in a garden or a field, whittling sticks with no particular end in view, is one of the most delightful, pointless activities a bunch of friends can share – and if you look on the internet, it will surprise you how many adults indulge too.

Elder pea-shooters and whistles

Find the right small elder branch and by carefully pushing out the pith you can make a pea-shooter, or even better, and historically sound, a pith whistle (*left*).

Cowboys and Indians

From larger straight branches we occasionally worked together to make our own versions of totem poles, using our precious, permissible penknives to

To make a bow

Find a bendy-but-not-too-bendy sapling branch and bend into the required shape. We needed string, of course, that essential for so many childhood activities, and a reliable way to fix it to both ends: the penknife came in handy here – most of us, if we had one at all, had the simple one-bladed sort with a colourful marbled handle which the blade slotted back into, sharp enough but hardly dangerous as it did not lock into place – a notch in the end of the stick, married with a groove carved round an inch or so from the end, gave sufficient purchase to anchor the string firmly enough. The second end was much harder to secure than the first, as the bow sprang to life and wouldn't be restrained and it sometimes took two of us to strong-arm it into submission.

create wondrous patterns in the bark, which we imagined were clearly akin to those danced round by Red Indians – we hadn't learned to say Native Americans then.

We were of course addicted to games of bows and arrows, not least because my parents forbad any semblance of guns – as I did with my children in turn, probably only driving them to use their friends' out of my sight.

Feathers were of course necessary for the flights of arrows – but how to fix them on? Shafts for arrows were quite easy to find in the hedgerows or domestic bushes but fletching them (lovely word, and how satisfying to recognise the origin of the surname Fletcher!) was something else. We kept hens sometimes, so at least their feathers were available although we looked for longer ones if possible. If anyone in our circle had been bought an Indian headdress we could plunder the brightly dyed feathers if they had tired of it; another use for feathers on another day, making our own headdresses and whooping around the neighbourhood.

If we had collected sufficient feathers for at least a quiverful of four arrows, fixing the feathers on became the puzzle. We used string, glue, rubber bands, cotton thread – and nothing worked. The feathers fell off, or guided the arrows straight into the ground. It was fun trying but as often as not our games of outlaws and sheriffs or who-could-shoot-the-furthest were happily enjoyed with un-fletched arrows.

When two of my grandsons were little and I was entrusted with them for some hours, I would sometimes take them onto Stourbridge, one of Cambridge's many wonderful commons, the site of one of Europe's largest mediaeval fairs granted to the Leper Hospital (still in existence) by King John. All we did, though, on this historic site, was look for feathers – magpie, pigeon, even seagull – and stick them in our hair. Properly adorned, we stamped rhythmically across the common together shouting *We are the Feather People! We are the Feather People!* to the beat of our steps. I think we puzzled the cows and horses grazing freely around; they frightened us a bit because they were so big. My now over-six-foot grandsons remember this today with some embarrassment but it was fun at the time.

Part of my childhood brought collections of a more sinister kind, although not sinister to us – man's inhumanity rather than nature's bounty. We collected shrapnel or pieces of rusty metal we were sure had come from a crashed German plane, although they were more likely to be from old farm machinery or a wrecked car.

Of course, being well taught, we did NOT collect birds' eggs or nests – I could never find any anyway, not even just to look at.

131

WINTER

Some ideas for winter

- Making camp fires
- Snow angels
- The snowman
- Saluting Mr Magpie
- Bird tables
- Pine cone bird feeder
- Quill pens
- Teasel hedgehogs
- Playing Five Stones
- Cairns and arrows
- Greeting wreath
- Potato prints
- Yule log
- Christmas table centre
- Pine cone trees
- Amazing space

Winter arrived. The seasons were more separate and defined then, I'm sure, or why did we read and write so many 'poems' and descriptions of their clearly defined variety?

It wasn't just the snow – I'll come to that later.

I have always loved the silhouettes of trees when they have shaken their leaves loose from their fingertips. Their black lines against early evening sunsets draw fine-boned, exquisite patterns, with roosting rooks upright like fat exclamation marks and the occasional bundle of a raggy nest or a ball of that eerie plant parasite, mistletoe. The bleak beauty has something elemental, perhaps because trees out-live us and therefore seem eternal.

I was fascinated to find in books clear diagrams of winter trees which meant I could sometimes identify a distant tree by its shape and branch habit, without having to see leaves, nuts or fruit which would normally name a tree for me. I felt very knowledgeable. How beautifully the trees, especially the poplars, behaved.

arate trees (in all but one

181

n. Most trees lean
ems of shoots (see
ring to upper surface.

183

talica'
n high.

186

× euramericana 'Serotina'
25 m high. Many trees
ure below).
ol-shoots, leaves
d of rather

1a
2a
3a
4
2b

KEEPING WARM OUTSIDE

We had to keep warm so climbing trees was good, and racing round admiring our smoky breath. When we were old enough to use matches occasionally we would make a camp fire. I had been taught how to cut turf away carefully so that it could be replaced when the fire was out, the spot had cooled, sticks and ash had been carefully scattered and all litter was of course either buried or taken home again – those were the days!

Camp fires

I knew of two methods of cutting turf to expose a safe and un-damaging place for a fire: either a long cut down the middle of the fire site, with two oblongs of turf, painstakingly sliced underneath, rolled back to form an untidy swiss roll at each side, or a diagonal cross cut on the proposed area with the turf peeled back like un-making an envelope to expose a neat square of earth. If there were large stones nearby, a satis-fying fireplace could be built, with licked fingers knowledgeably held up to determine the prevailing wind so that a life-giving draught could be created.

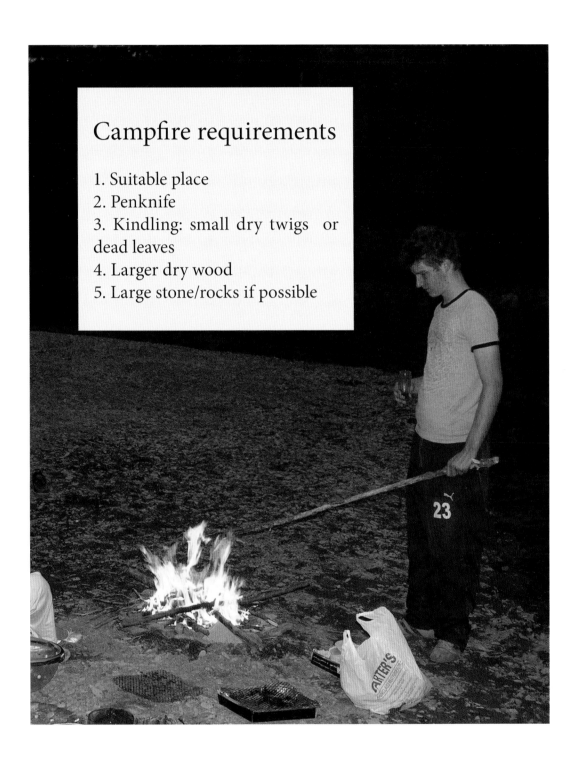

Campfire requirements

1. Suitable place
2. Penknife
3. Kindling: small dry twigs or dead leaves
4. Larger dry wood
5. Large stone/rocks if possible

Method

1. Cut lines in turf either X or H (Fig 1) and roll turf back carefully, slicing about 2 inches deep underneath to preserve roots (Fig 2).
2. If stones available, place round created earthy space, leaving channel for prevailing wind (Fig 3) – test for this with licked finger!
3. Place kindling first, then build open wigwam over with small dry twigs (Fig 4).
4. Light the kindling, blowing on flame if necessary to make sure twigs catch
5. Add larger and larger twigs then small branches over flames, either in wigwam style or in straight lines
6. If appropriate, potatoes can be pushed into ashes if fire has burned long enough and the flames have died down
7. ALWAYS – put out fire leave to cool, scatter ashes and stones, replace turf and stamp down firmly. Water the turf if possible.

IT SHOULD ALL LOOK AS IF NOTHING HAS HAPPENED

How to cut turf for a camp fire

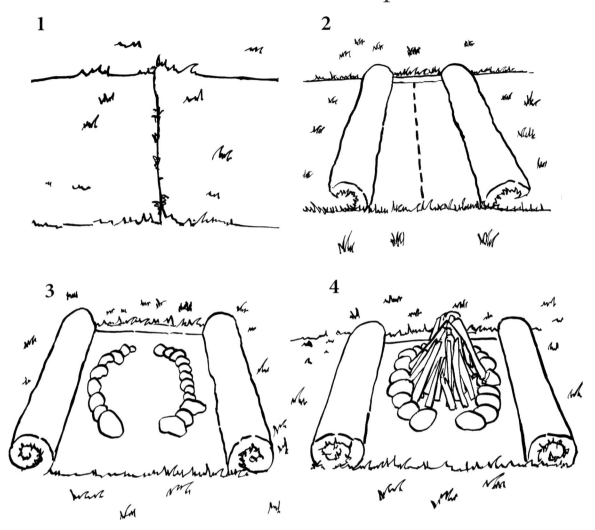

Baking potatoes

I think we sometimes scrounged potatoes and baked them in the ashes but I remember they were generally blackened yet uncooked when we lost patience and retrieved them too early, excitedly throwing them from hand to hand because at the very least they were hot.

SNOW

My most vivid childhood memory of snow is of looking up into the sky on dark evenings watching snowflakes fly and swirl through the light of the street lamp outside my house, a ceaseless strangely dark supply at that angle that was almost frightening and suffocating (was there enough air to breathe between them as they fell remorselessly down?), then looking ahead and down to see it immaculate white and to feel it settle on trees and pavement and houses and our clothes and my face. There is nothing more magical to a child.

Snow in my childhood came every winter so it was rare enough but familiar enough. Is it settling? How deep is it? Can I go out? Where are my wellington boots? Is it the right kind to make snowballs? Are all snowflakes really unique?

This clean, cold adaptable substance was ours; the white, quiet world was ours. If it snowed first overnight, the unearthly light on the bedroom ceiling gave us the news – it's snowing!! And nothing mattered but to get out in it, get with the gang and celebrate our best playmate. It was so cold. My woolly gloves became sodden and freezing so quickly. You learned to do without gloves, waiting for that moment when your icy hands glowed red and warm, as they always did after snowballing for a while naked-handed.

Wellingtons were a necessity but a problem: we girls hadn't reached the sophistication of wearing trousers when I was little so it was knee-length socks and warm skirts for winter and the problem was the gap – socks always fell down, despite desperate elastic garters under the turnover, or were too short and then the tops of the Wellingtons chafed, wet and scratchy, and each cold leg had a circle of red, raw chafe by the end of a snowy session outside. I would with difficulty turn the tops of the wellies down an inch or two to relieve the stinging, which only made a second line of red soreness. None of this stopped the glory of playing outside in the snow, of course.

Living in a quiet close, with not many neighbours owning cars in those days, most of our play was in the street, in our own private world, which must have been hilariously visible to adults, had we noticed. We did so many things: snowball fights and snowmen; eating snow from walls where it was

still pristine; finding un-trodden tracts where we could make the first footsteps; drawing and writing our names in the snow.

We had little in the way of slopes but my father did make us a sledge, of solid oak with brass runners which was indestructible but heavy!

I remember one snow creation we made traditionally each year, with no thought of our own or others' safety: collectively our whole gang (I was by chance the only girl in this bunch of similar-aged children who lived down our road) made a long, broad slide of packed, iced snow down the middle of the top end of our road, stretching past four or five houses.

We took it in turns to career down it, the most agile 'performing' and showing off gloriously and hilariously as they went down. It must have been so dangerous for the few car drivers.

Walking in a snow scene on your own as a child had a different kind of magic. It was always so quiet, often the only sound being the crunching of the snow packing under each footstep. Everything looked so different, transformed – the grass, a branch, the roof. I remember feeling something like awe seeing birds' delicate footprints on virgin snow in my own back garden. If it was cold enough, a spider's web traced in ice between two twigs on a bush was exquisite.

I assume children brought up in the country would have the added magic of animals' footprints in the vast snow of fields and moors, and they could learn which animals had made them and perhaps what they had been doing to make the marks in such a place and in such a way. Even the footprints of a domestic moggy or pet dog look exotic across untrodden wastes of new snow.

Snow angels

I hadn't seen the simple game of snow angels until I saw my primary school age children suddenly lie flat on their backs on a smooth patch of good snow and whirl their arms and legs up and down like those clowns on sticks where you pull a string to jerk their limbs; the children would scramble up and, lo and behold (appropriate language indeed), there would be a perfect angel-shaped dent for each whirling child in the snow, wings and all.

How to make a snow angel

1   Find surface covered in smooth snow
2   Lie down flat on back
3   Wave arms and scissor legs up and down flat on snow
4   Carefully stand to see angel in snow

Winters seemed long, with multi-coloured Christmas in the middle. We couldn't play out for long and, unless it snowed, we couldn't find much to do together outside, when we'd exhausted football and hopscotch.

FEATHERED FRIENDS

My parents usually fed the birds that visited our back garden, especially in the winter, so I became familiar with the most common ones. The birds kept moving, so I couldn't become as close to them as I was with trees and flowers and bugs but I loved their freedom, their total lack of interest in humans, ignoring us as far as possible; I felt they had no conception of who or what provided the peanuts or the water – hey, they're just lying around so let's eat 'em!

I found myself watching especially the 'pretty' birds – chaffinch, robin, the tit family, greenfinches (*right*). I liked the sparrows, flocks of them in those days, but felt some sympathetic fondness because they were so plain and dowdy. I learned to look for the starlings' iridescent speckled backs when they descended in flocks onto the garden, fluttering down like scraps of brown silk, quarrelsome and greedy, as acrobatic as the tits in getting food from hanging feeders. If you've put bread in the garden for birds you can tell starlings are there by the scraps flung in the air as they voraciously pull a crust apart. I am saddened and amazed to learn that today the numbers of starlings and sparrows have diminished, as well as some songbirds like the bullfinch and the song thrush.

Even our prettiest birds are modest and vulnerably small.

> *A robin redbreast in a cage*
> *Puts all heaven in a rage*
>
> William Blake

Just occasionally I would see a brightly coloured woodpecker and marvel at the staccato noise and rapid drumming as it made a hole in a tree trunk – how could it move its neck so fast the image was actually blurred? I came to realise we naturally enjoy watching the more colourful birds like an attractive, interestingly-dressed human draws more eyes and comments than the quieter, more dowdy 'sparrows'!

Morning Mr Magpie

Magpies have always fascinated me. I loved from a child their dramatic black and white (which isn't, on closer look) and their manic chattering call. The strong black beak is almost menacing, and the long wedge-shaped tail feathers give it a distinctive flight pattern. Superstition surrounds this magnificent bird and I eagerly learned to salute if I saw one and then call the following greeting, on pain of bad luck if I didn't:

'Good morning/afternoon/evening, Mr Magpie, how are you?
And how are your wife and children?'

There seems to be continuing debate about whether magpies are partially causing the diminishing numbers of native songbirds; knowledgeable people argue convincingly on both sides. I have watched blackbirds happily pecking away on a lawn, running and hopping, calling to each other and their fledglings, go silent and still as a magpie flies low overhead. I've watched the same (probably) blackbirds 'mob' a magpie as it got too near a nest of eggs or chicks, dive-bombing, driving it away by collective effort, despite being much smaller.

The size and dramatic appearance of magpies, their intelligence, mimicry and eccentric behaviour have given them a high profile. Children learn to count their sightings of these wonderful birds (I am slightly biased because I support a certain North East football team…) and excitedly look for resulting happenings:

One for sorrow
Two for joy
Three for a girl
Four for a boy
Five for silver
Six for gold
Seven for a secret never to be told.

Magpies are from the rook family, corvidae, with the wonderful genus name of *pica pica*. I was never very good at remembering classifications of plants and animals, despite a love of Latin at school; I much preferred the local common names for things.

However, the discovery that another of my favourite birds, the cheeky and diminutive wren, had been imaginatively labelled *troglodytes troglodytes* still makes me smile with delight.

The big black birds

Rooks, crows, ravens, jackdaws – my only means of distinguishing at least two of these genetic siblings is the following helpful saying:

A rook by itself is a crow,
A crow in a crowd is a rook

but it only applies, apparently, when they are roosting.

Like all children, I remember being awed by the formidable majesty of the ravens, huge and black, at a visit to the Tower of London and trembling to learn The Tower and the Country would fall if there were fewer than six ravens resident at the Tower! The pageantry of a Raven Master serving among the Tudor-dressed Yeoman Warders (always Beefeaters to children) was so beguiling – I'm not sure what I think about it now.

a crow in a crowd is a rook

Television has shown us exotic birds from other nations: tiny enamelled jewel-like humming birds, bower birds creating an attractive framework for a possible mate, birds of paradise dancing their display rituals, flocks of pink flamingos, peacocks and vultures, condors and penguins – once I could see a coloured tv, long after childhood, I marvelled at them but always cherished our quieter domestic varieties. The small screen has also shown us vast flocks of our birds migrating, of puffins clowning about on the cliffs, cherished golden eagles and ospreys and tiny chicks new-born in nests.

I have never been a proper bird-watcher, a twitcher with a list and a pair of binoculars, or any good at recognising their songs but the birds are there, the books about them and the internet are there, and children can learn to love and observe quietly these free-flying, singing, nesting fellow-citizens. I taught myself as a child to recognise a male or female blackbird even from a distance by watching them flirt their long tails up as they land. I have seen a ghostly barn owl quarter a field at dusk, and a thrush crack a snail open on its anvil stone.

Unlucky feathers

Exotic peacock feathers, which on the whole as far as I was concerned, had to be bought, although gloriously beautiful did not feature in our world – and were reputedly unlucky to bring indoors so were no use as decorations anyway.

BIRD TABLES

A bird table in the garden is relatively easy to set up, or feeders hanging from trees, with some provision for water – it is a delight to watch a dusty starling have a splashy bath in water you have provided, or a thirsty robin scoop up water and throw its tiny head back to let the water run down its throat. The RSPB gives copious advice on the best ways to maintain garden birds. The enemy is the grey squirrel – but what fun to watch one sit up with a piece of apple in its tiny hands, nibbling away, bright-eyed and bushy-tailed.

Pine cone bird feeders

A pine cone can form the perfect base for a home-made bird feeder. A large one, warmed until it opens its spines, can be filled with a tasty mixture involving porridge oats, suet or lard or even peanut butter, and birdseed or any other beak-some morsel you can conjure up. Hang it in a tree or from a bird table and the tits and finches will flock.

Equipment
1. Large pine cones
2. Crunchy peanut putter
3. Some kind of fat, like bacon
4. Something basic like flour, porridge oats
5. Birdseed and/or breadcrumbs
6. String

Method
1. Mix peanut butter, basic element and fat
2. Push mixture firmly down in between cone scales all over cone
3. Cover with birdseed/breadcrumbs
4. Harden overnight
5. Tie piece of string to top of cone or among top scales
6. Tie to tree branch or bird table

Quill pens

Of course all children know about quill pens and Shakespeare scratching away by candlelight. It dawns at some stage that's why we have the word pen-knife. As always, the internet provides learned and detailed information and instruction about quill pens, their origin and construction.

A quick approximation to authenticity can be achieved by begging from a neighbour a goose feather, if you have the right kind of neighbour, or finding any long-ish tail feather from any large bird.

The shaft of the feather is hollow and by carefully cutting a small slanted section off the bottom, then splitting the resulting 'nib' a short way up the middle, you will have a very scratchy, spluttering quill pen, to dip in ink (if your household has any – unlikely in these days of biros and felt tips and fibre tips and gel pens…) and write your Petrarchan sonnet.

You could add bogus legitimacy by staining paper with a tea bag and roughing the edges to look like parchment.

Making a quill pen

You will need

- A long-shafted feather, like goose, turkey, swan – or any long feather, say from a magpie, you pick up in the garden
- A sharpish penknife or craft knife
  – BE CAREFUL!
- Liquid ink

To make the pen

1 Strip off some of the feathers, leaving a clear length at the 'nib' end. Some people strip off the whole of one side
2 Cut off the tip at a sharp angle (Fig 1)
3 Make a slit up the tip of about ¼ inch (Fig 2)
4 Shape a 'nib'
5 Pen is now ready to dip into ink and write master pieces

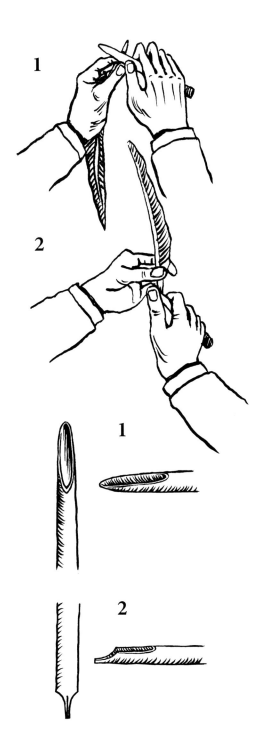

Teasing teasels

This beautifully architectural plant is only teasing in its spelling – we could go with teasel, teazel, teazle or teasle for starters. The spiny bracts of the distinctive dried flower head in autumn swirl round in another of those fascinatingly mathematical designs perhaps based on the so-called Fibonacci numbers like the sea-shell – these are worth learning about, especially if you're interested in the language of numbers, which I could never grasp but appreciated from a distance. (The numbers start 0, 1, 1, 2, 3, 5, 8, 13, 21 etc)

The patterned, spiky head of the teasel was used all over the world to tease-out or raise the nap on woollen cloth during manufacture and at a

pinch could be used now for those wretched bobbles that disfigure our jumpers.

As a child, I was awed by tall, elegant teasels, perhaps because I didn't see them very frequently for some reason. I can see they would make good combs for long dolls' hair (or even pet cats' fur, very, very carefully) but I only made one thing from them, apart from more recently using them in a vase as a wonderful decoration just by themselves.

Teasel hedgehog

One possible artefact is a teasel hedgehog. Find a good-sized teasel head, wearing gloves if you are of a sensitive nature. Break or cut off the stem so that just enough is left to create its snout – yes, the stem's the front end. You need black-headed pins or tacks to poke in (ouch) for two eyes and the snout, or you will need to paint the conventional gold drawing pin heads into the beady shiny black that befits this snuffling creature.

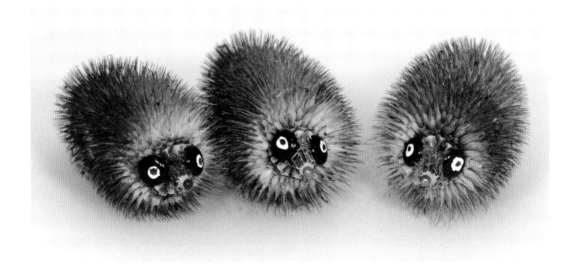

Latter-day knuckle-bones

On a mild winter's day, we used to crouch in circles to play Five Stones, a game which I believe has many different names around the country.

I must make it clear I don't mean Jacks, that hugely inferior game played with bouncy balls and sometimes small metal sputniks. No, five stones is the honoured descendant of the ancient (Egyptian? Greek?) game of knuckle bones – though whose bony relics they played with I dread to think. Five stones is normally played with five different-coloured clay 2cm cubes but it can be played almost as well with five small flat pebbles picked up wherever you happen to be. That's all you need, apart from a flat-ish surface and your more skilful hand.

You can play by yourself or with any number of others, although just one other is probably the best to keep the game going at a good tempo. Same-sized dice make quite good substitutes but they are usually very lightweight.

The basic move is to pick up all five stones with one hand and throw them into the air, attempting to catch them all on the flattened back of your hand which you have hurriedly turned over while the stones are in the air. The stones which land safely on the back of your hand are tossed into the air again, from there, and caught in the same hand. The stones which may initially miss the back of your hand create the next moves, although you must catch at least one.

If you drop them all you are out. It all sounds so complicated but it isn't, truly! Every group of players creates their own variations but most start with the plays called onesy, twosy, threesy and foursy, where the stones dropped from the initial throw are picked up in ones, twos, threes or fours (or however many you have dropped) while one stone which you have tossed up is in the air and must be caught, after you've picked up the one, two – all with only one hand…

And that's just the very basic beginning! A game can go on for hours or for five minutes. The different plays or throws are so arcane, so detailed and so complicated we have given them an entry of their own, on pages 161 and 162.

I have such clear memories of playing five stones, with the clay products or with pebbles, throughout my life – on carpets, wooden floors, pavements, fields, playgrounds, sand, earth, moss, playing fields and concrete – anywhere will do. I have played with pupils, siblings, friends, enemies, children and grandchildren; I still love the game – perhaps because I am quite good at it.

Instructions for Five Stones

1. Find five small flat stones of similar size
2. You need to be sitting on the ground with a area of flat surface between you and your opponents

It is essential to learn/practice the basic moves before trying the variations of the game (see opposite).

Cup the five stones in your better hand (left-handed, right-handed) and throw them as a group in the air, far enough up for you to have the time to turn over the same hand to catch them on its flattened back. It doesn't matter if you drop some as long as at least one is balanced on the back of the hand.

If you drop them all you are OUT
Any stone/s balanced on the back of the hand are now tossed into the air and caught in the palm of the same hand.
If you drop even one you are OUT
Each time you are OUT your opponent/s get their go.

You need one of the stones you have tossed up and caught, the jack stone, so discard any others.

Throw this stone in the air and pick up one of the dropped stones while it is in the air, then catch it in the same hand so that you have two stones in your hand. Discard the picked-up stone. Repeat this with all the dropped stones, one by one.

Five Stones variations

Here are some variations, which can be played in any order after number 7

1   Onesy

As above, the basic moves

2   Twosy

As above, except the stones on the ground must be picked up in twos, previously placed together, while the jack stone is in the air. With an uneven number the last stone can be picked up by itself

3   Threesy

As above, but in a three

4   Foursy

As above, but in a four or as many together as you dropped

5   Open Onesy

As above

6   Open twosy

As above, except you must not place the two dropped stones together but must pick them both up from wherever they landed while the jack is in the air

7   Open Threesy, Foursy

As above, not placing the fallen stones together before tossing up the jack.

8   Creeps

Throw and catch the stones as before. Any dropped stones must be picked up between your fingers while balancing the one/s you caught on the back of your flattened hand. Toss up the balanced ones and catch them, then ease the stones from between your fingers into the palm of your hand to join the ones you caught. If you drop any you are OUT

9   Crabs

As Creeps, except you bend down your fingers like a crab to pick up the dropped stones between the tips

10 Under the Bridge
    As before, except each dropped stone must be knocked by
    the throwing hand one by one under a bridge made by your
    spare hand on the ground while the jack is in the air
11 Over the wall
    As Under the Bridge, except each dropped stone must be thrown
    over a wall made by your spare hand on the ground while the jack is
    in the air
12 Sweep the Floor, Dust the Table, Put the Baby in the Cradle
    As before, except throwing hand must pretend to sweep the floor, dust a
    table, and picking up the stone put it into the palm of the spare hand,
    with three throws of the jack in the air, one for each action.
13 Slamdunk
    As before, but each dropped stone must be dropped through
    a basket ball ring made by your spare hand high off the ground
    while the jack is in the air
14 Score a goal from a free kick
    As before, but each dropped stone must be 'kicked' from where it
    lands by flicking the forefinger of the throwing hand, through
    goalposts made by your spare hand
15 Little Titch
    As before with Onesy, except each stone is retained in the hand
    when it has been picked up, ending up with all of them in the hand.
16 Big Titch (my favourite)
    As before with Onesy, except ALL stones caught on the back of the hand
    are thrown up as jacks and caught, then the stone picked up is added
    until all four stones are thrown up as jacks to pick up the last one.
It is possible to invent any number of variations, and anyone reading these
will have their own.

MORE STONE ACTIVITIES

Creating cairns

Stones demand to be picked up! Over the centuries, even over the millennia, people have picked up stones to throw for fun or in anger, to make houses and walls, tombs and barriers. It is easy to build a very simple but effective landmark by piling stones into a cairn and it has become a custom to carry a stone to the top of a hill and place it in a pile at the summit to mark the successful ascent. Cairns are surprisingly moving when they mark human endeavour or human tragedy.

Tell tale trail

Carefully shaped small cairns can be used as patterans, as can a tied tuft of long grass or specially laid sticks – all can leave a vital message for someone to follow your trail through uncharted territory. I learned this 'secret' skill, wonderfully useful when tracking each other in elaborate Wild West bad-man hunting or snow-bound trapping games, again from the perennially wonderful and useful *Swallows and Amazons* books.

NATURE'S OWN CHRISTMAS DECORATIONS

Of course winter means Christmas above all to children. The build-up was much less commercialised when I was a child and didn't start in the shops in the summer as it seems to now! The excitement and enjoyment were much more concentrated into the last few weeks, leading up to the heart-thumping magic of Christmas Eve and stocking-hanging, and then the great day itself, carefully spread out by my parents by only allowing presents after Christmas dinner, eaten at about 2pm usually. So we had to wait until we'd helped to clear away and wash up before the ceremony of the substantial present-giving began, which meant we were still pleased with them by bed time.

We helped create the excitement and move the day nearer by making Christmas decorations with anything we could lay our hands on. Some we could make largely from our nature treasures.

The holly and the ivy

Whenever I have lived near enough to a wood or at least an open space with trees, I have always loved to collect festoons of ivy and graceful branches of holly, well-berried where possible. They are so traditional, so beautiful – and so easy to drape over picture frames and mirrors or round banisters. Occasionally I have been lucky enough to find an untidy bundle of parasitic mistletoe high up in a tree so that we could have a provocative bunch in the hall; more often we had to buy some from a market stall or greengrocer but it still had its other-worldly aura.

Greeting wreath

I think I have just made that name up but I always thought the custom of hanging a Christmas wreath on the outside of the front door to wish season's greetings to neighbours and passers-by was such a friendly gesture. Even a child can have a good stab at making one. The base can be ivy, holly, laurel or any other evergreen branch bent round to form a circle and secured with string, which can also provide the loop for hanging the finished wreath. It can be decorated with anything you choose – baubles, tinsel, streamers of red ribbon all look festive and can last the twelve days or so that they may be hanging up outside in wind, rain or snow.

To make the greeting wreath

You will need
A bend-able length of evergreen, such as holly, ivy, laurel, fir
String
Red ribbon, baubles, tinsel, balloons – any decoration you choose

Process
1   Bend the length of evergreen into a circle of the size you want your wreath to be
2   Carefully secure with string. You could leave a loop at this stage to hang up the wreath
3   Decorate with eye-catching Christmas colour – holly, baubles, tinsel etc. Make sure they are firmly fixed on
4   If wished, tie a big bow of red ribbon. The ribbon can also be used to tie the wreath to the front door instead of the string
5   Fix carefully to front door

Original wrapping paper

You can hardly call a potato a nature treasure, unless you grew it yourself I suppose, but with a few potatoes, some cheap white shelf-lining paper and some poster paints, children can make wonderful wrapping paper – and keep quiet for hours! A potato sliced in half, with a Christmas star or simple Christmas tree shape, for example, cut into the flat surface, can be used again and again, covered in bright paint, to print a pattern over the white paper. Endless variations and designs are possible and family and friends will be especially grateful to receive presents wrapped in hand-painted Christmassy paper; its very crudeness will add to the appeal.

To make hand-printed wrapping paper

You will need
Large potatoes
Vegetable knife
Sheets or roll of white paper
Powder or poster paint
Glitter if wanted

Process
1. Cut a potato in half across the middle
2. Cut a raised design into each flat surface – ie. Christmas star or tree or any simple shape
3. Cover the raised pattern with paint
4. Print onto the white paper, in a repeated pattern
5. Add further designs from other potato cuts as wanted
6. Glitter can be sprinkled on while paint is wet if required
7. Leave to dry

The Yule log

Although there are many apparently well-documented theories on the origins of the yule log tradition, no-one seems to agree on the origin of the name itself. However, since most western households now have central heating or, at the most, a gas or electric fire flickering away with artificial flames, there is little scope for a real burning log, lit from a charred remnant preserved from the previous Christmas to ensure continuity of life and well-being.

However, small pretend Yule logs make excellent table decorations and are easy to create. You just need a log which is self-stabilised by a side twig or which you could flatten a bit underneath so that it doesn't roll at a crucial moment. Clearly, it needs snow – cotton wool, talcum powder, soap powder, caster sugar – anything will suffice; if you can add glitter, so much the better.

The log will provide a wonderful stage for your pine-cone owl, or your teasel hedgehog, with small sprigs of holly to add festive delight. Of course, your Yule log may well have to compete for attention with the nowadays popular chocolate sponge-cake variety.

To make the Yule log

You will need
A small attractive log
White substance to create a snow effect – cotton wool, soap or talcum powder or even artificial snow if your pocket can run to that.
Glitter
Objects to decorate log – pine cone owl or tree, holly sprigs, teasel hedgehog

Process
1   Make sure the log is stable and will not roll.
2   Create the snow-topped effect, adding glitter if wished.
3   Glue or securely balance your chosen decorations, dusting them with 'snow' if appropriate.

A Christmas table-centre

You may need to beg a few things from the grown-ups for this, as well as using your own gleanings from the woods and fields. A family round the table for a special meal – great place and time to show off your skills! Basically, you are creating a colourful, attractive centre for eyes to rest on in the (relatively) orderly chaos of Christmas dinner.

It can't be very tall, or people will not be able to see their fellow-munchers. The base can be a large plate or bowl, a flat basket, or even a decorated box or tin – anything to act as a safe container. Our ever-useful pine cones look wonderful, just piled in as a gorgeous background colour and texture. They can either be left in their autumn brown or painted, sprayed or glittered.

What else have you collected, dried? Teasels, dried poppy heads, leaves, seeds, grasses can all be used, perhaps sparingly, either au naturel, or coloured or gilded. To ensure the Christmas touch, holly provides shiny leaves and scarlet berries.

On the begging-from-grown-ups front, small fruit like satsumas or grapes add colour and shape; if possible, a few candles, firmly and safely fixed in holders, will look especially wonderful and professional, with a couple of tree baubles completing the glittering spectacle.

To make a Christmas table-centre

You will need
A large plate, shallow basket or bowl, box or tin
Collected or dried objects such as pine cones, teasels, ears of corn, seed heads. These can be gilded, glittered or painted as wanted
Sprigs of holly
Baubles, candles, tinsel, fruit as required

Process
1   Arrange a firm basic collection of pine cones, fruit
2   If you are using candles, make sure the holders are firmly embedded in the basic collection
Decorate your centre-piece, remembering to keep it low so that people can see over it easily

Pine cone Christmas trees

Pine cones are magical creations of nature: they look and feel so special. They can be collected and admired as they are, they can provide aromatic fuel for an open fir or be turned into cunning artefacts.

A fine fat pine cone is tree-shaped already, pointed side up. Sticking its base into a small nest of cotton wool balls can stabilise it, as if deep in a 'snow drift', or it can be glued to a log or a cotton reel 'tub'. Painted a good strong dark green, it will look elegant with glitter or artificial snow sprinkled on while the paint is wet.

There are so many possibilities for decorating your tiny tree, depending upon your ingenuity and creative skills, but beads, sweets, scraps of tinsel, paper candles and crackers can all attractively and successfully mimic the full-sized version.

To make the pine cone Christmas tree

You will need
A full fat pine cone, sufficiently open to have a good shape with 'branches' – warming will open a tightly furled cone
Green paint
Glitter if wanted
Appropriate decorations – beads, tiny sweets, paper stars, scraps of tinsel, miniatures from Christmas crackers etc
A base – cotton wool balls, cotton reel, small plastic top or tub

Process
1. Paint the cone dark green
2. Sprinkle with glitter or 'snow' if wanted
3. Fix firmly onto a base
4. Decorate as you wish

Finally...

I have lived for more than two thirds of my life under the over-arching splendour of the fenland sky. Our planet is glorious and muddy and fun and instructive but we are tiny. How can anyone write about the sky? I know little of planets and galaxies and black holes and anti-matter but I know when I look up into the stars on a clear, frosty night, when I'm far enough away from urban sprawls to avoid light-pollution, I feel dizzy, over-awed by the moon and the stars, off off into space and beyond. Try it for yourself – sit in a field, lie back, go quiet for five minutes then whisper:

Star Light Star bright,
The first star I see tonight,
I wish I may, I wish I might,
Have the wish I wish tonight

The earth and the sky are always changing and always achingly familiar to us if we stop and look and marvel and love. Walter de la Mare explained our relationship with nature in his short poem 'Night':

That shining moon, watched by that one faint star:
Sure now am I beyond the fear of change
The lovely is in the familiar
And only the lovelier for continuing strange

I believe we should as children become so familiar with the world out there that we realise how strange it is.

The snow disappears, the ice melts, majestically
the year turns again and again it is spring.
Full circle.

INDEX